A MAN'S FEELINGS

Red San Publishing

PO BOX 284, Bellevue, Washington, U.S.A.

www.redsanpublishing.com

www.audiostoriesclick.com

www.bookondivorce.com

First published in 2008 by Red San Publishing.

Library of Congress Control Number (LCCNs): 2008924569

A Man's Feelings: Finding Closure After Divorce/Michael L. Eads—1st ed. / edited and with an introduction
by Bob Olson.

ISBN-13: 978-0-9798484-3-8 ISBN-10: 0-9798484-3-1

DESIGNED BY BING YANG

Printed in the United States of America

2 4 6 8 10 9 7 5 3 1

To Mom and Dad ... miss you

A MAN'S FEELINGS

Finding Closure After Divorce

Michael Louis Eads

Red San Publishing
Bellevue, Washington

I don't measure a man's success by how high he climbs but how high he bounces when he hits bottom.

— *General George S. Patton*

CONTENTS

PREFACE

IVORCE; A WORD SYNONYMOUS WITH FAILURE, disappointment and heartache. Any man who loved his wife and went through divorce feels the stigma and loss. The courts use these words: dissolution, irretrievable and broken. These heartless terms create turmoil to a man going through divorce. Going through this crisis, I found my own identity and self-esteem in question. Divorce forced me into a crossroads where my judgment and sanity were compromised.

While I was going through the hardest times, I felt like a child lost in the woods just out of range of my mother's hearing. I also felt alone, scared, ashamed, embarrassed, but mostly abandoned. My innermost weaknesses were exposed. Divorce does not discriminate, it knows no boundaries. The brand divorce leaves on a man can be indelible.

RELAX; THERE IS HOPE. With time, patience and work you can reach a better place: A place of healing, happiness and closure. I learned the importance of closure when I was only six years old. After my separation and divorce, my need for closure was reinforced.

How do you make it to that place? Through my mistakes, I chart a path, a roadmap that can help any man going through this calamity. You will know you have arrived at your destination when "the old you" is no longer recognizable and a new man is born. When you have acknowledged your mistakes and let go of the past, you will realize your potential for a bright future. You will have achieved closure. So give yourself a pat on the back for wanting to feel better. Remember, it is going to be okay.

INTRODUCTION

I'VE KNOWN MICHAEL EADS SINCE HE WAS A TEENAGER. He is a no-nonsense man who has led a hard life while maintaining integrity and good judgment. His story is exceptional, yet the challenges in his life apply to the challenges any man or woman faces enduring emotional despair from divorce.

Divorce derails life. The word "divorce" from his wife hit Michael like a wrecking ball. He never saw it coming. His marriage was flawed, but so was that of his parents, and most marriages he knew. His parents coped with conflict. They didn't "just give up." Not so with Michael's wife; she "gave up" and her decision was final.

Michael's struggle to recover was long, painful and plagued with setbacks. He was lonely, depressed and burdened with erroneous advice from friends and relatives. He felt "Unless you're in my shoes how can you understand?"

I believe with the raw personal expertise of an everyday man, Michael's story is unique and uplifting. His advice is straightforward and insightful, offering hope and encouragement on the long road to find a new life for any man struggling for happiness after losing the love of his life. I recommend this book for every man and woman in despair; it truly provides a road to redemption.

Bob Olson

A Man's Feelings

Finding Closure After Divorce

ONE

DOS (THE END)

I WILL NEVER FORGET THE DAY and where I was when my wife, Connie, said she wanted a divorce. It was June 10, 1996, a Monday, at 5 p.m. How and why she arrived at that decision remains a mystery, but that is no longer important to me.

I was at home; she came in the front door and said, "I want a divorce."

"Why?" I asked, looking at her in disbelief, "You don't know what you're saying, you're just upset about something I did."

I realized this was real when she shook her head and said, "NO, I want a divorce!" The tears rolling down her face and the look in her eyes were clear indications of her sincerity.

How did it come to this? I pondered that until it no longer mattered, or at least did not have the credence it once did. The important thing to note here is, I did not see it coming. Connie did. The questions were: How long did she want this? Why did she want this? I will never know the complete answer. I recovered from it, and with time, the pain eased and the healing commenced.

In case you are wondering, DOS stands for "Date of Separation"—the most important day in my life. I do not care about the day of my divorce, because by the time it went through the courts I had already accepted it was over … forever. The DOS is vital because on that day the affection, love, tenderness, kissing, caressing, and love-making ended forever. Okay, I hugged her once a year later when she graduated from college. One hug, and from my point of view that seemed fake, but she asked for it, so I gave her a pretentious hug.

I was three weeks from turning thirty-five and had been with her since I was eighteen, almost half my life by that time. Can you imagine how it feels to have all that affection taken away in one day? Yes, we were having sex on a regular basis and doing the intimate things married couples do, but she was hiding something, and I did not realize it. After that, I was a walking zombie for about three months. I was literally in shock!

This became apparent when a customer I had for ten years, Mrs. Kristianson, called me and asked why I had not been out there to service her lawn. I told her I would come tomorrow but not today. She said—and I will not forget—"Mike, are you all right?"

"I'm okay; I will be there tomorrow," I gave her a good long pause and lied. This woman (God rest her soul) was "old school" and felt my pain coming through the phone line.

This was one week after Connie told me she wanted a divorce. I remember waking up that day. Something was terribly wrong. I did not realize it at the time—I was having a breakdown.

I called my wife to tell her I was falling apart. She could tell because she started crying. Michael Eads never says he is falling apart unless he really is.

I gently pulled apart the drawn shade and looked outside. The bright melancholy sun made me think, "I am not going anywhere today ... nowhere!" Even though it was a nice day, almost summer, I could not walk out the door. I was in shock and would stay that way, albeit not as bad as that day, for the next three months, until I accepted this was real and I would never be the same.

I pleaded with her to see a marriage counselor with me, to find out if our marriage could be saved. Do you know what I got from that experience after over *thirteen years of marriage*? About *thirteen minutes,* and I had to really ask for even that much.

"If she wants out, then it's over," the counselor said repeatedly.

The marriage counselor did ask an interesting question. She asked, "If you had the chance to marry Connie today, would you do it?"

I said, "I will have to think about it", because I felt it was a difficult question to answer, especially when she wanted out. Connie, on the other hand, gave a resounding "No!"

"The question isn't difficult, answer it," the counselor stated. I told her she was rude. I would not be pressured into any rash answers.

Years later, I realized the counselor was right, but she could have been more compassionate. I felt my thirteen-plus-year marriage was worth more than thirteen minutes. Nevertheless, my soon-to-be ex and that callous counselor did not.

DISCOURAGED, I WENT to see my longstanding Doctor, Joe Boardman, for advice. As I was venting my frustration, I told him, "I don't know, Joe, marriage is just not what it used to be." His wise response, "Yes, Mike, but the real question is; what did it use to be?" I believe my parents' generation was more accountable within their marriages than subsequent generations. Joe also referred me to a therapist, which I recommend to all men facing separation and divorce.

THE DOS, DATE of separation, is a very important date to note and remember. The emotional and legal ramifications are enormous. I actually had to look up the date of my divorce to write this book, whereas the DOS has left an indelible impression in my mind, because on that day my marriage ended forever. Therefore, in almost all cases, DOS equals the end!

TWO

CAN THIS MARRIAGE BE SAVED?

I KNOW WHAT YOU'RE THINKING: "He just gave me a long lecture on DOS and 'the end,' and now he's asking me to work it out."

Yes and no.

I am simply asking if the marriage can be saved. If it can be, you will save yourself (and her) much grief and heartache. If you have children, you really need to try to work it out. Children typically blame themselves for a divorce, and you must make every effort to avoid this. Think of the pain you will save them if you can resolve differences and save your marriage.

Both of you should see a marriage counselor if you are having problems. Find out what the issues are so both of you can work on them. "Work" sounds like you're punching a clock and greeting a boss every day. Yet, do not be as I was and assume if one person wants to work on it, the marriage will magically work out. It will not. If either party does not want reconciliation, then it's over.

You need to take a good look at each other, and your marriage. Remember, this was the woman you fell in love with and pledged "forever to" in wedding vows. She should be special to you and hold a warm place in your heart. She should feel the same way about you. A healthy marriage is based upon love, understanding and trust.

In a healthy relationship, both people need to agree on vital issues. It's okay not to want to try some of the time; however, if you or she feels that way all of the time, your marriage is in serious trouble.

There are so many reasons why people fight. For us, the biggest were money, control and jealousy issues. Connie had the serious jealousy issues. I remember when we sold the house and were parting forever, she came to me and said, "I'm sorry I was jealous and so often accused you of having affairs, when I knew you weren't. My own insecurity made me do that."

"Why in the hell are you telling me this *now*?" I responded. By then, I had come to realize this divorce was actually a good thing, whereas it was an impossible concession for me to make just one year earlier.

Connie wanted a divorce and I still do not know how she arrived at that decision. Her official reason was, "I don't want to try anymore." When she gave up, the marriage effectively ended. I know it sounds cruel, but it does not matter why one person wants out, because when this happens, it is time to separate.

I often hear people say, "We just stay together because of our kids." I guess they assume their kids like to see two grown-ups arguing and bickering with each other. If your kids are old enough, they will never forget, and may never forgive you for treating their mother badly. There is nothing harder on children than seeing their parents fight all the time. If the marriage can be saved, do it. But if either party is unwilling to compromise, it's time to move on. Once you determine it is unworkable, you need to pick up the phone and call the best attorney you can afford. Do it today.

THREE

THE STIGMA OF DIVORCE

O N MY COMPUTER DICTIONARY, "stigma" is defined
as follows:

*Sign of social unacceptability, the shame or
disgrace attached to something regarded as socially unac-
ceptable.*

Wow, that is exactly how I felt after I was divorced. I
felt like The Biggest Loser and this was way before the TV
show of the same name.

The divorce went through on January 6, 1997 (two
days after my dad's 66th birthday). The reason I mention
my dearly departed father is that he was the

only person, on either side of our families, who told me to try to work it out.

I remember signing the petition for dissolution of marriage about three months after she came to me with the news. I called my father and he said, "Are you going to work this thing out?"

"Dad, it's over."

"Son, but the time investment, both of you have made on this marriage, is too much to give up."

Sometimes my father could be so right; this was not one of those times. I told him divorce was not my decision. I had done everything I could to save our marriage, but she said, "No."

"Accept it, Dad; I have."

It took me over three months to acknowledge it, and I realized there was no going back. He knew how upset I was. "What will you do now, Son?"

"I don't know, but I must learn to live with it and without her."

What did her family say? Not one word, at least not to me. It took me a while to figure out why. Now, I believe they knew a long time before I did. I was the last one to know. I felt humiliated and ashamed, the last one to know, but the first loser.

It was as if her family was saying, "This is business as usual." Our families had completely different views on commitment and marriage. My family believed once you are married you stayed married. I grew up Catholic and divorce was just plain wrong. Even though I no longer participate in the Catholic Church, I still respect the sacredness of marriage. I would not give up just because "I didn't want to try anymore."

Connie grew up with a different outlook. Our parents were poles apart in their respective beliefs. Connie believed if you fail at something, that is it, you quit. My dad told me if you fail at first you try harder until you know for sure you are a failure.

We were like many couples who marry young; we were very different and that became apparent even before we got married. We lived together for two years and it was a rocky road. We fought and made up constantly. Because we truly loved each other in those early years, we decided to get married. Actually, she decided we should get married. I felt we still had some growing up to do. After all, I was only twenty-one and she was twenty.

I recall being approached by her pastor at the church we were attending (we were going to her church at the time). He said, "Mike, I have a compatibility test I would like you and Connie to take."

"Why? I'm not going to take that silly test."

"Just humor me and do it."

Well, we both reluctantly agreed to take the test, and it was quite a revelation.

"Before marrying, both of you will have to work on these things." He sat us down and proceeded to give us a rather lengthy list of the problems we might encounter if we were to marry. On completion of the test and after examining the results, I realized the Pastor knew exactly what he was talking about. Not only did he pinpoint problems we were already having, he would also be a soothsayer in the fact that almost all of our subsequent problems were brought out into the light because of that test.

Recalling all these events helps me now to understand where and when things went wrong. They also help me avoid the same mistakes. Remember that old saying: *Those who don't learn from their mistakes are destined to repeat them.* It's true.

FAST FORWARD TO the first year of my divorce (1997): A loser, a failure, lonely, worthless, and just plain low. That is how I felt in those early months, and I know many of you may feel the same way.

Divorce is like someone dying. Yes, dying. It says on the petition for dissolution of marriage: *"This marriage is irretrievably broken."* Damn, that's harsh! You don't hear that word "irretrievable" every day. It sounds final, doesn't it? I realize now there could not be more appropriate words for the end of a marriage: *"irretrievably broken" and "dissolution of marriage."*

Dissolution sounds like Robert E. Lee talking about the end of the Union. He used that word, but he was talking about the Country, and we are talking about your union or marriage, which is now dissolved. In the eyes of the courts, they are merely appropriate terms to use; to me, they were incredibly final and absolute in tone and meaning.

I felt like a loser. Yes, put a big "L" on my forehead and brand it there. And I was convinced everyone, especially women, could see that big "L." Then holidays roll around and the person whom you have been going to all these functions with for years is suddenly gone. How did that happen? All the married women wanted to know how I was doing, which I interpreted as, "How much are you suffering, Mike?"

It felt odd how people looked at me, people who knew

me my entire life. I just "knew" when they looked at me they saw that big "L" right there on my forehead. "Don't say anything to upset him, honey. Can't you see that 'L'?"

As if that isn't bad enough, society labels divorced people. Nothing is off limits; everything, from your credit to a simple job application. Everyone wants to know if you are divorced. I suppose I am old-fashioned when I say, "It's none of their damn business."

Then the advice comes: What you should do and where to go to meet women. The advice is coming from people who have not been on a date since they used their feet to stop the car. I will go into that later, but it is important to remember not to listen to those who have no idea what you're going through or how you feel. What you must realize is you are not alone, and all divorced men must undergo a transformation from what you were to who you are now, and who you will become. It takes time, but you will feel better.

FOUR

NO FAULT MEANS YOU'RE SCREWED

I RECENTLY FINISHED WATCHING A SERIES that originally aired on HBO called "Rome." I was surprised how many times they mentioned divorce. Divorce in the days of Caesar? Yes, it seems the concept of divorce is very old, indeed; Then I googled the word "divorce." Over 114 million hits. Wow! The "D" word is a very popular subject.

I proceeded to go to www.wikipedia.org and found some interesting facts. I strongly suggest you do the same. Please note: Wikipedia is constantly updating information and the following statistics are based upon the time I reviewed them on August 8, 2007. However, it would be a good idea for you to check Wikipedia for current information. As of August 8, 2007, it said:

"In the United States, in 2005 there were 7.5 new marriages per 1,000 people, and 3.6 divorces per 1,000, a ratio which has existed for many individual years since the 1960s. As many statisticians have pointed out, it is very hard to count the divorce rate, since it is hard to determine if a couple who divorce and get back together in that same year should be considered a divorce, so there is in fact no predictive relationship between the two annual totals... Nonetheless, the claim that 'half of all marriages ends in divorce' became widely accepted in the US in the 1970s, on the basis of this statistic, and has remained conventional wisdom."

The point here is that many marriages, for whatever reason, do not work out.

. . .

HISTORY OF DIVORCE

WIKIPEDIA WENT ON to say:

> "*Divorce existed in antiquity, dating at least back to ancient Mesopotamia. The ancient Athenians liberally allowed divorce, but the person requesting divorce had to submit the request to a magistrate, and the magistrate could determine that the reasons given were insufficient. Although liberally granted in ancient Athens, divorce was rare in early Roman culture. As the Roman Empire grew in power and authority, however, Roman civil law embraced the maxim, 'matrimonia debent esse libera' ('marriages ought to be free'), and either husband or wife could renounce the marriage at will.*
>
> *The no-fault divorce revolution began in 1969 in California, and was completed in 1985 (the last holdout was South Dakota). However, New York does impose a mandatory separation period before a divorce can be granted.*"

God bless New York.

WHAT DO YOU think happened to the divorce rate after 1969? More importantly, who do you think initiated the divorce after that? It's all right there; in 1975 just six years after that historical 1969 date, women filed a whopping 71.4% of the cases.

According to Wikipedia:

> *"In their study titled 'Child Custody Policies and Divorce Rates in US,' Kuhn and Guidubaldi find it reasonable to conclude that women anticipate advantages to being single, rather than remaining married.*
>
> *When women anticipate a clear gender bias in the courts regarding custody, they expect to be the primary residential parent for the children and the resulting financial child support, maintaining the marital residence, receiving half of all marital property, and gaining total freedom to establish new social relationships."*

In other words, women could have half of everything men have worked for all their lives just by saying "I want out!"

In the great state of Washington, where I live, I can become rich through a lifetime of hard work and toil, get married and have half of *everything* I own taken away forever! Connie and I split everything up as best we could, or should I say, she could. I was not in a clear state of mind when I signed those papers. That was my fault. I should have had an attorney examine the papers. So again, if you have not done so already, call the best attorney you can afford because if you're in a no-fault state like Washington, the odds are in her favor. This is especially true if you have children together.

Based on Wikipedia:

> *"The no-fault divorce does not need a fault as a cause. Common reasons for no-fault divorce include: incompatibility, irreconcilable differences, and irremediable breakdown of the marriage."*

"No-fault divorce" is a legal term for the convenience of getting divorced. In reality, there is no such thing as no-fault divorce. You, your spouse, or both of you, or possibly something undefined, caused the marriage to break down.

When Connie came to me asking for a "no-fault divorce," I was in shock and humiliated and wondered, "What did I do wrong? How could she walk out on our marriage like that without any explanation?" I felt like a piece of torn merchandise or a pair of her worn-out shoes, something to be discarded. On the other hand, as in "no-fault," she can take back her clothes to the store with a return policy by telling a cashier, "Nothing wrong with it, I just changed my mind, don't want it anymore." Yes, like the marriage: "No fault ... I don't want it anymore."

Harsh words for intimately bound human beings' lives; a man with feelings, who is trying to understand what went wrong; a man who was raised as she was; a man who values his pride, sense of worth, and sense of responsibility to his family. I need to be treated as a human being, not merchandise.

I was brought up with the beliefs that you fell in love, got married, and spent the rest of your life loving and caring for that person. That's what my parents did. Every couple has issues and problems; it's part of life. When Connie decided to quit, I felt helpless. I could not simply accept my marriage was over without trying. I wanted to work on it. Connie did not. She "didn't want to try anymore."

If your wife asks you for a divorce, do not automatically point the finger at yourself alone. I can tell you from experience, there will be many unanswered questions. Remember: You are only responsible for your part of the failed marriage; you are not the whole cause. If you accept this now, the divorce process will be easier and recovery faster.

Divorce can change people. Women are not bad people, nor are they our enemies. They look at things like money, property and power differently than men. If they get the advice of a good attorney, you can be assured they will do everything they can to protect what they feel is theirs.

FIVE

MY EX AND MY MISTAKE

I T WOULD NOT BE FAIR IF I DIDN'T AT LEAST tell the story of how my ex-wife and I came to be. How we met is the most bizarre part of the beginning of our relationship. I used to live near a nice lake by a busy road. My parents' house was at the bottom of the steep hill that intersected the busy road, 15400 block of SE 21st Place. I went through my adolescent teenage years there, so it's safe to say this is where I went through the biggest changes of my life. There the paramount change happened when I met Connie. And it goes without saying that neither of us were the same afterward.

My father expected me to do my chores in a timely and orderly fashion. He served with the Army in Korea and always bragged he did his basic training near the great general George Patton museum out of Fort Knox, Kentucky. Not getting the work done in my father's eyes meant you were either gravely ill or dead. The man accepted *no* excuses.

One of my chores was to check the mail every day, Monday through Saturday. I would walk up the steep hill to the mailbox and back down to deliver the good or bad news to my parents. Each way I would pass a yellow house, and I often wondered who the new owners were. I had gone to junior high school with the previous owners' son, but we were not friends.

IT WAS 1980. I was having a fun and crazy summer. I was hanging out with Billy Wade, one of the first friends I made in this not-so-small town called Bellevue, Washington. Billy epitomized the word "cool." He looked good doing almost everything. We smoked our first cigarettes together, talked about girls we hadn't met, and boys we didn't beat up. We could fight, but neither Billy nor I would admit which one of us was tougher. Billy would not act as if he was better than any of his friends—that wouldn't be cool. We boxed on the same team at the Boys Club and Billy was faster with his fists. He couldn't outrun me back then, but he had the reflexes of a cat and would always go around catching flies. Billy was funny and like me, a rebel. We understood and respected each other.

Billy had a girl-catching car, a chrome-adorned, 1970 sky-blue Camaro. When we would cruise in his car, I hoped the girls might notice me by the company I kept.

One nice day, right at the start of summer, we were cruising near our old school when I noticed a girl with long blond hair playing tennis. "Let's go watch them play," I suggested.

It was Connie. She was playing a slow game with her little sister, Terri. We sat watching the ball, I mean, her hair, bounce back and forth with the ball. Finally, I said to Billy, "Maybe we should go over there and say something."

"You say something," Billy said.

So, I yelled over to them to come on over to the car, and before you knew it she was talking to me on the passenger side of Billy's car.

The second thing I noticed about her, besides her hair, was her steel-blue eyes. Billy later commented on those eyes and how they seemed to look right through you. We talked and laughed. I asked her where she lived.

"Oh, not too far from here," she said.

"Where?" I asked.

"Over by Phantom Lake."

"What?"

"Yeah, over there on SE 21st Place."

Surprised, I responded, "I live on SE 21st Place, too."

We looked at each other in disbelief. Then, I asked her, "Where on SE 21st Place?"

"Just two houses up the hill in that yellow house."

"How long have you lived there?"

With a coy look on her face, she said, "Three years."

Remember my getting our mail every day? Based on what she was saying I had walked by her house twice a day, six days a week for three years and never saw her, not once. Her younger sister, Terri, did look a little familiar, and I definitely did recognize her youngest sister Lisa, but I had not seen Connie. She said the same thing about me and had no idea there was any guy her age living in my house.

I was eighteen; she was seventeen when we met on that fateful day. We were still kids. As you can imagine, once I found out where she lived, things changed quickly and dramatically. After that, I made it my personal quest to win her over and make her mine. Too bad—I was the only one to feel that way. Connie seemed to have little interest in me. Incensed, I wanted her more. It took some doing, but I finally persuaded her I was a boy she needed to get to know better.

In some ways, Connie was the female version of me; loud, aggressive, argumentative, and to the point. She loved to party, and she had a few boys chasing her. I seemed to be last on her list, but that changed.

BEFORE TOO LONG, we were going places and doing dangerous things together. My parents did not like Connie at first and now I can understand why. They saw her as "nothing but trouble." Her parents liked me, especially her dad. I felt at home at her house. I don't think Connie ever felt at home with my parents.

What most amazed me about her parents was how young they were. Her mom was thirty-seven and her dad was thirty-nine when we met. They looked and acted young. My dad was almost fifty, and he looked it. My mother was in her late forties. I felt like Connie's parents were part of my generation.

Then we started hitchhiking together and having fun.

With Connie, we always got a ride. Next, we started sneaking over to each other's houses at night, which I made into an Olympic event. I worked swing shift at an insurance company and got off some nights at midnight. I would go home, wash up, and sneak out my bedroom window. I lived in the basement of a split-level house. My parents and little sister were upstairs, so it was easy to get out while they were sleeping. The only problem was that initial opening of an old bedroom window without waking anyone. I soon mastered that by opening it a smidgen in advance to avoid clatter in the wee, quiet hours of the morning.

Then I would hoist myself out and take the long journey—"thirty seconds" to her house. Tap, tap on her window, and I was in. But it was a lot harder getting inside. The reason, her father never seemed to sleep. I could always hear him up there and felt he sensed my presence. Connie had the exact same visiting setup as mine, except my parents actually slept.

THIS CONTINUED UNTIL the fall when I made the biggest mistake of my life. Connie would be a high school senior then, and I was drudging along at my job as a night watchman. It was almost Thanksgiving when Connie asked if I wanted to "take off."

"You mean leave?" I could tell she was planning something crazy.

"Let's take off and go somewhere."

"You mean somewhere around here?" I could see the answer on her face. Connie wanted to go somewhere very far from here.

"Let's go to Florida," she suggested: About as far as you can possibly get from Bellevue, Washington, in these Unites States.

I realized she was serious and putting me in a no-win situation. Florida didn't seem like such a bad idea. My brother, Chris, was stationed in Pensacola, so we could show up and give him a nice surprise. He was nearing the end of a four-year enlistment, and if we went, I would want to say "hello" before he got out of the Navy.

Off we went. It was the night before Thanksgiving, a Wednesday. Could there be any worse timing? Our mode of transportation—thumbs. We hitchhiked, and that was the next mistake. We went to Seattle, because I figured it would be easier to get a ride to another major city if we stuck our thumbs out near a freeway ramp. It worked. A trucker heading to Spokane picked us up. That was the direction we needed to go, east. In fact, no cars ever picked us up, only the "big rigs." That was the route we took. We would be let off at truck stops in order to get another ride to our destination. It was fun until we came to that long and lonely state with the big sky.

IF YOU HAVE not been through Montana, then you cannot understand how long and lonely that state is. I had been there in the past, but had not driven from one end to the other. While in Spokane, we hitched a ride with another trucker and he said he was going all the way through Montana. We smiled and got on. This trucker was quiet and said we could sleep in the back if we wanted to. Connie and I welcomed a much-needed rest.

When we awoke, things looked the same. I wondered: "Does this state ever change?" It was so bleak and flat compared to Western Washington. We were riding along when the trucker abruptly pulled over and said, "You two need to get out."

"Why?" I had no idea where we were and there was not a building, house, store or gas station in sight.

"Both of you need to get out NOW!" he said one more time.

I remembered what my father said about truckers and my previous experience with them. They are a strange lot and almost all of them carry guns. I had already seen this guy's gun so I grabbed Connie and said, "We have to leave!"

It was a crisp, clear, and cold November morning. We looked down a stretch of open road that seemed to have no end and no cars or trucks. We needed to get a ride. Every time a car happened along we would stick out our thumbs, but no one ever stopped. Montana must be the most unfriendly state in the union for hitchhikers. We walked for miles, and with every step, I kept saying to myself, "It's so cold."

Hours later we found a place to eat. I asked the waiter where we could find a place to stay for the night.

"A ways down the road," she responded.

Great, more walking. I didn't bother to ask anyone in that restaurant for a ride. I could tell by the look on their expressionless faces, the answer was "*no.*"

It was almost dark when Connie said for the first time that day, "I'm cold." I had not mentioned it because I didn't want her to know I was freezing all day. We finally reached a small motel and rushed inside. I could see another *no* on the face of the front desk clerk. Perhaps she could read a clear, "I'm going to kill you if you say no" expression on my face. Reluctantly, she gave us a room.

Connie and I had our first good night's sleep there; after that, things got even more bizarre.

FOR FIVE DAYS, we would be picked up and let off by different truckers and sometimes things went okay, other times not. We made it to Mansfield, Ohio, over 2,000 miles from home. We were exhausted and needed sleep. We went to an IHOP and fell asleep on the bathroom floor with the door locked. That lasted ten minutes until someone knocked on the door.

Then we decided to get some breakfast. I noticed two men taking a particular interest in us, with persistent staring. They looked like cops to me, but Connie thought I was paranoid. It was obvious we were from the road. We had bags and suitcases. I was certain they not only noticed us, but also could tell we were not from anywhere around there.

We grabbed our things, went out the door, and walked awhile, but I felt watched. Connie grew restless as we walked through a park. She stuck her thumb out to get a ride. I knew this was a mistake. I could see a car and felt those cops watching us. Sure enough, they approached us and asked, "What are you doing?"

"Trying to get a ride and who wants to know?" I

answered nervously.

The curious man responded, "It's illegal to hitchhike in any public park in Mansfield. I am a police detective and this is my partner."

I realized immediately our odyssey was over.

"Can I see some identification," the detective with the thick black mustache asked.

"Yes Sir." I handed over my ID. The last thing I wanted to do was aggravate them. I was cooperative and polite. Connie stood there, and didn't say a word.

Looking at our identification, the first officer replied, "Bellevue, Washington—you two are a long way from home."

"Is that by Seattle?" the other detective inquired.

"Yes, it is Sir," Connie finally spoke up.

"It looks like you're seventeen, young lady," the thick mustache cop said.

"Almost eighteen Sir," she replied, "in six weeks."

We would have been let go, but they had to check if she was a runaway. Sure enough, Connie was listed as missing. Then they got very interested in me.

They separated us and asked Connie if I forced her to come with me. She confessed it was all her idea and she really "kidnapped" me. The younger blond detective came to me and said, "Well, Mike, it looks like you're free to go. We didn't believe you did anything wrong."

He thanked me for being cooperative and asked what I was going to do. I replied, "I'm staying with her because she's scared and I love her."

This cop seemed proud of me and said, "I knew you would protect her."

After that, we joked and laughed about how we were in the restaurant, looking at each other wondering. "I knew you guys were cops the first time I saw you."

"How?" the young cop asked.

"He always knows," Connie added.

Driving to the bus station, they kept going on about Mount St. Helens. They asked where we were when it erupted. Anyone old enough from Seattle remembers where they were on May 18, 1980. They seemed obsessed with the eruption. I told them the big local saying was, *"Where were you when the mountain blew?"* That got a few more chuckles. For me, now, that date has tragic significance as my sister died May 18, 1993.

It was a real pleasure being busted by those two polite cops. Dropping us off at the bus depot, the mustached cop made me promise to take her back home. "You have my word on it Sir." We said our goodbyes and got on that old Greyhound bus for our long ride home.

THE BUS RIDE home took three long days. On our way back, I looked at Connie and told myself, "This was a huge mistake."

One funny thing happened, which still embarrasses me. Connie was bored and feeling sexy. She asked if I wanted to join her in the rest room. This bus was loaded with people and they would know something was up if we both went in there. She said, "I'll go first, you wait five minutes and come in."

My obvious response, "You don't think anyone will notice that?"

Connie won.

We were young, strong, and made a lot of noise. I was caught up in the moment and the embarrassment that followed. When we went back to our seats, I tried to keep a straight face. A large, loud black woman looked right into my eyes, so I knew there would be trouble. She spoke in a loud voice, "I KNOW WHAT YOU BEEN DOING IN THERE! I HEARD THE POUNDING, MOANING AND THUMPING!" Everyone on the bus heard her. They all started laughing including the bus driver. The woman continued, "I DON'T NEED TO BE HEARING 'THAT' BECAUSE I WON'T BE GETTING 'ANY'

FOR ANOTHER WEEK!"

My face turned red and Connie could not stop laughing. That was about the only funny thing that happened on our trip. When we arrived home, things were not so funny anymore.

MY BIG MISTAKE

WHEN WE ARRIVED at the bus depot, her parents were all smiles. It did feel good to be back in Seattle, but I wondered if my parents even knew I was home. I called them that first night from Spokane and they were not pleased. Before we left my parents and I were not on good terms. My father and I would fight constantly, and my mother had become a stranger to me. I felt this trip would not be such a hardship for them.

This turned out to be one of the biggest mistakes of my life. My mother was so hurt and humiliated she would talk about it until her death, some twenty-six years later. My father, a man motivated by pride, hid his feelings better, but I could tell he was crushed. Since I felt unwelcome at my house, I moved into Connie's home and felt welcomed there.

SOMETHING HAPPENED THAT signified how my life was back then, which still hurts me unbearably. One gloomy night, Connie and I went for a walk. On our way, we had to pass by my parents' house. They had a dog named Annie, who was raised from a pup. I spent a lot of time with her and I loved that dog. My dad was taking her out to potty when we were walking by and Annie saw us. Excited, she got away from my father and ran across the street. A car happened along and Annie ran right under it. She died in my arms.

I brought Annie over to my dad who looked at her and said, "I'll take care of her." Dad grabbed a shovel and mom asked me to come over. She was crying for me to come back. Dad said, "No, I'll take care of it." I still have the haunting memory of my dad walking aimlessly with that shovel and my mother crying in our doorway. I will never forget it. After that, things were different between my parents and me. It is difficult to describe the change, but there was a change. All this is to prove my love to a selfish seventeen-year-old girl.

THIS CHAPTER IS dedicated to all the young men who might be reading. If any girl ever asks you to choose between her and your parents, walk away. I can tell you from personal experience that *no girl* is worth the grief that your parents will go through, if you do something as stupid as I did. I lost a good job, my home, and a great deal of respect from my parents, all because I did not have the guts to walk away. Besides, do you really want to be with a girl that wants you to make a choice like that?

No! You do not.

Did anything good come out of this? A lot did, actually. I made a stand against my father and became a man, which was long overdue. I eventually moved back in with my parents for a short period before I was on my own for good. I was too young and inexperienced to know the ramifications of my behavior.

My parents and I later enjoyed a great relationship, but this took a long time to develop because of what I did. To become my own man, I felt I needed to make a stand. I realize now I could not have picked a more inappropriate way to do that. My mother died while I was writing this book and it is her inspiration that guides me. My impulsive mistake of running away with a teenage girlfriend broke her heart. It took me over twenty years to say I was sorry because I did not fully understand how much I hurt her.

After my father died, I visited my mother on Sundays. Every so often, she would bring up what Connie and I did. I offered no excuses, "What I did was wrong, Mom. I was wrong, and if I could take anything back, it would be that." May God bless you and keep you safe my dear mother. I will always love you.

CONNIE AND I would move in with each other. Eventually my parents forgave our immaturity. Some of you may be wondering why I married this girl after our inauspicious beginning. I loved her and I felt we were meant for each other. We were young, and sometimes foolish. We started to visit our parents more often because they lived so close. We were deeply in love in those early years and I can remember her running into my arms to greet me after a long day of work. Things change fast when you are that young.

Connie and I had many good years, and I respected the sanctity of our marriage. Nevertheless, I cannot help but wonder what would have happened if I had said no to that trip. My life could have turned out differently, or it might have turned out worse, who knows? However, it would have been my life and not one molded by an ultimatum from a seventeen-year-old girl.

When I made the decision to marry Connie, I took my wedding vows and our marriage seriously. I was raised that way and that is the primary reason this divorce was so hard for me to accept. Marriage was my decision and I take full responsibility for it. No one forced me down that aisle and I was too naive to know what I was getting into.

When we got married I was the same age as my father when he married my mother, so if it worked for him, why not me? Things did not turn out as I expected, and I have learned to accept this.

I forgave Connie a long time ago, not so much for her sake, but mine. If you carry around too much anger and bitterness throughout your life, it consumes your soul and can make you a sad and lonely person. Love and forgiveness are the greatest gifts of humankind. They are the two things we all can do.

SIX

.

KIDS WILL NEVER FORGET: CUSTODY BATTLES

LOOKING BACK ON MY MARRIAGE AND DIVORCE, I am grateful Connie and I decided not to have children. We discussed having kids but could not agree on how we would raise them. I believe our decision was a responsible one. I am by no means an expert on this subject.

I know several men that are going through the dilemma of having to say goodbye to their kids just for the privilege of paying their ex-wives child support, and they all are so bitter about it. All men should be required to pay their fair share. It is the unfairness of having infrequent custody of children they love just as much as their former spouses do that leaves a sour taste.

I have seen their kids suffer, and that makes me very sad. Why is it children are made to suffer so much in this life? Many parents worry about their kids shaming them, but never blink an eye when they shame their kids. Make no mistake, kids feel ashamed, guilty, and perhaps the worst feeling ever, abandoned. They feel anger, bordering on hatred. Strong feelings become visible in a kid, and they are real. Children of divorced parents may slowly forgive, but they will never forget.

What do parents do? Too often parents use their children as pawns against one another. This is inexcusable. These people are behaving in hypocritical ways. They talk about how much they love their children while using the very same children to serve their own agenda. Many parents are into having kids, but fewer are into raising them. With so many kids and more divorces, my generation of "baby boomers" has to be one of the most selfish.

Do you remember when you were a kid? I do. I used to cry when my parents fought. All I can remember thinking is I wanted them to stop. Just STOP! Sometimes they would really shout at each other, and we kids would have to stay quiet and listen. It was in those hushed moments I vowed never to get married. I did not ever want to say hurtful things to someone I loved. So what did I do? Grew up, got married and fought with my wife, precisely as my parents did. Sometimes you make promises you just cannot keep.

Children have very good memories. You must be careful what you say and do, especially in regards to their mother. Do not forget she is their mother and *always* will be. You will make yourself look mean in their eyes if you argue and shout at her. So stop and put some distance between you and your ex-wife when you are irritated. Besides, you will not solve any problems by arguing for argument's sake. Don't make a mistake you can't take back.

If you are in a divorce and custody battle, remember to hire the best attorney you can get. There are few benefits for a man in a divorce other than his release from an unhealthy marriage. On the other hand, there are countless benefits for a woman, especially in a no-fault state like Washington. A friend with whom I swim told me, "A woman can marry more money in a minute than a man can earn in a lifetime." This is the true meaning of the phrase "double standard." I believe it is essential for every man to take great care with legal aid, going through every step of separation and divorce to protect his interests and that of his children.

SEVEN

KARLA'S LAST WORD

I REMEMBER GROWING UP IN the Wallingford district of Seattle when I was a little boy. There always seemed to be something going on. We kids were everywhere. The Hanovers had eight; my parents had six, and so on. We were the last of the baby boomer generation and we were out to have some fun.

I loved to play Army with my two older brothers, Joe and Chris. You could buy an entire bag of Army men for a dollar and kill each other all day. One day a little girl with bleached blond hair, showed up. Her name was Karla and she was a remarkable sight. Although I never told her, I liked her the first time I saw her. I think she liked me too because she would come over almost every day and ask my mom if she could play with me. We did everything together, and I was becoming fond of my new friend.

Whenever I was playing with my brothers or friends and Karla would walk by, they would all say, "There goes your girlfriend." I would say, "SHUT UP, SHE'S NOT MY GIRLFRIEND!" Or was she? I had to admit I felt a little proud when they would say that. So I suppose you could call Karla my first girlfriend.

I knew we were different but I couldn't understand why. I seemed to be dirty all the time while Karla was always clean. She always wore a dress. Pink, white, and blue, and for some reason, I really liked her in that blue dress. She smelled good and always smiled and told me she was my girlfriend. When we were alone, she asked me if I wanted to be her boyfriend, and I said yes because I felt like I was from the first time we met. I was six and she was five; we were the youngest kids in the neighborhood. Actually, one kid was younger but he was only three, still a baby to other kids.

All the kids in the neighborhood would play in our back yard. Karla and I had a hiding place where we could go and watch the other kids play. It was under my back porch and a place that only small kids could crawl into. We would hide in there and watch the others play through the lattice. No one seemed to notice us. We had our own special "kid time." It was our secret spot and where Karla told me she loved me and wanted to marry me someday. She also asked me to kiss her, so I gave her a six-year-old sloppy kid kiss. I remember holding her hand while watching the other kids and thinking: I was so happy to be with this pretty friend—*my girlfriend.*

ONE DAY, I was playing a serious game of Army with my brothers; Karla showed up and really wanted to talk to me. I shouted at her, "CAN'T YOU SEE I'M PLAYING ARMY? LEAVE ME ALONE!" She started to cry and left. My brothers even said, "That was mean."

The next day when Karla did not show up at my house to play, I asked my mom where she was.

"Didn't she tell you, Michael?" (My mother always called me Michael.) "Karla moved away yesterday. She was trying to say goodbye."

So many feelings ran through my mind and body. I shouted: "KARLA MOVED AWAY!"

I immediately ran to her house, which was a block away, but for me at that age it seemed like a mile. I pounded on the door! No answer. I knew then my mom was not lying. Karla, my first real girlfriend, was gone forever. Gone, and I *never* got a chance to say goodbye. It was my fault, after all; she did try to say goodbye to me, but I told her leave me alone, which was exactly what she did.

So that was it, no more Karla. I missed her every day for what seemed like months, but actually, was only weeks. It's amazing how fast you move on as a kid. Yet, I still felt bad about not being able to say goodbye.

A few months later my mother asked me if I wanted to go to Northgate Mall, a real mini-Disneyland for a kid like me. I was mad at her about something, so I said, "NO! I'll just stay home." I had four older siblings, so someone was always there to take care of me.

When she returned, she said, "Guess who I saw at the mall, Michael?"

I knew the answer, "YOU SAW KARLA!"

"She says 'Hi' and that she misses you," Mom said.

I cannot forget how mad I was. Another chance to say goodbye and I blew it again. Karla said she missed me too; another low blow to my already bruised ego. I was mad awhile and then sad. I started crying.

"What's the matter, Michael?"

With tears in my eyes, I replied, "I never got a chance to say goodbye and I yelled at her too."

My mother looked at me, smiled and said, "It's okay, Michael; Karla knows you miss her too."

I didn't say goodbye and I never saw her again. I felt there was no closure.

AT THIS YOUNG age, I learned how important it was to achieve closure. I strongly recommend doing your best to accomplish this. Face your ex-wife and tell her you are sorry for your part of the failed marriage. Watch the look of astonishment on her face as you apologize. If she is rude or mean, at least you have created some closure for yourself. Then it will be her problem, not yours any longer.

Karla's last word combined with my unspoken word will always haunt my memory. Even so, as an adult, I can find closure by admitting my mistakes and being a man about it. Remember, the true measure of a man is not how much money he makes or how many things he possesses. What defines us as men is respecting our parents, loving our family and friends, and admitting when we are wrong.

EIGHT

RE-SINGLED, REST, RECOVERY AND ROUTINES

Your divorce has gone to the courts and you are now officially re-singled. What will you do? That is exactly how I felt the first year in my long and confusing journey through divorce.

My advice: take a deep breath and relax. Your marriage is over.

It's time to accept this. Learn some things and move on. This is no time for major decisions, especially if you feel angry or depressed. If you're having a difficult time, get professional counseling. You will recognize some things about yourself and your divorce you cannot, or will not, see alone. I am not embarrassed to admit professional counseling helped me. Alone time can be a benefit; however, using your pride as a shield to force yourself into isolation is unhealthy. You are not married any more, and it's time to call yourself "single," not divorced.

Why?

Two reasons: First, if you walk around calling yourself divorced, then you're calling yourself a victim. Second, you are single now, just as you were before you ever met your ex-wife. To all available women, you're single and it's time you started acting that way.

I remember meeting a girl not long after my divorce. She told me to my face, "Get a clue, Mike, you don't even know if a girl likes you because you act so married." She was right. I was so busy talking about my ex and failed marriage that I didn't even notice if another woman liked me. I was surprised she liked me in that way. Consequently, I missed out on some real opportunities. Another woman doesn't want to hear about your broken marriage and ex-wife. The woman you're with deserves your attention. Talk about anything but the "D" word or your ex.

.   .   .

DO YOUR LAUNDRY

WHAT DO YOU do now? Whatever you want or feel like. Take up a new hobby or write a book. Start a business, go on a vacation or take a much-needed rest. You are free and although it may feel strange, you need to find a way to enjoy your freedom.

I took a lot of time to rediscover myself. I felt like a child again, reviving my youth and wondering where this journey would take me. I was alone and scared, but somehow felt I could get through this. Take this time to find a way to heal and do some serious soul searching. Problems are a lot like laundry, you must sort them out, one at a time.

Remember, the first few months, and in some cases years, after divorce are a vulnerable time. Abstain from bad habits and addictions, as this will only exacerbate your problems. Never try to solve one problem by creating another.

If you have a hobby or passion, then by all means, pursue it to the fullest. It's okay to have routines and a schedule, even if you think they're tedious.

. . .

IN MY FIRST year after divorce, I had the most boring schedule you can think of. Now, I realize that schedule was a blessing.

It's up to you to find out how long you need to recover. Remember, a divorce can be as hard on you as the death of a loved one. Do not be influenced by people who tell you how long it should take. It takes as long as you need and not one minute less. Try to discover the new you. Realize there is life after divorce. It will not be the same life, but for all you know, it might be a better life.

THE FIRST SUMMER of my divorce I did the same thing almost every day. I would wake up at 9 a.m. and watch an episode of the old sci-fi classic, "The Outer Limits." I had, and still have, a landscaping business, so I could set my own hours. Believe me, I did. I would watch my show, eat my breakfast until 10 a.m., and then put on a side of one of my favorite albums, "Eat a Peach," by the Allman Brothers. I still had a turntable and albums because I loved the nostalgic touch of putting that "needle in the groove." I listened while I cleaned my kitchen and started my day.

Then, I would shower and head out the door. I worked until about 7 p.m. and went to the pool. Lap swim was from 8 p.m. to 9 p.m., Monday through Friday, and it would take a major earthquake to make me miss that. After my swim, I would go to a local Boston Market and order the same thing nearly every day, chicken and mashed potatoes or ham and beans. Everyone there knew me so I felt right at home. After dinner, I would go home, watch a late movie on HBO, and go to bed.

The sameness—I did just that almost every single day the entire summer. Saturdays I would go to the afternoon swim, which is the swim I do now. That's it, day after day; exactly the same thing.

One day I cleaned the vinyl siding on our house and didn't wear rubber gloves. Well, it burned my hands real good. I went to see my doctor, and he said, "Mike, you should take a few days off to allow your hands to heal."

"And miss my swim! Are you *crazy*?" He wasn't, but I was. I put every waterproof band-aid I could get my hands on, and went straight back to the pool. The chlorine did not feel good on those newly burned hands, but I totally refused to miss my swim.

The water became my comfort zone and I needed that swim. I would jump in the water and let all the air out of my lungs as I went to the bottom. I still try it sometimes; it's fun. I felt all the stress coming out of my body. That was the only time of day when I felt in control. I was a distance runner for years but at that time, I had a nagging foot injury that would not heal. I had to swim! I had so much taken away from me, and as long as life was in me, my swim would not be one of them.

I ONLY WENT on two dates that entire year, 1997, and one of the girls complained I reeked of chlorine. Proudly, I stated, "Well, I think that's better than reeking of cigarettes." A smoker, she looked at me and didn't say a word.

The other girl smoked but was also a swimmer and didn't complain about my chlorine musk. It turned out we had a lot in common except for smoking and that she drank too much, and always lied about it. It's easy to catch people who drink too much in lies. They can't remember the shit they do when they're drunk. I don't understand how some people can be drunk, shit all over someone else, and then sleep like a baby. Alcoholics can, without blinking an eye. Then, when they black out from excessive drinking, their minds go to sleep. It's scary being around someone who does not remember what you did together the night before. [My mother passed away while I was writing this book. I must apologize to her for using the "S" word, as she detested swearing. 'Sorry Mom—there is no better word for what self-centered alcoholics do to people.']

If you are recently divorced and having some trouble staying focused, I suggest having a firm schedule and sticking to it. Throw in physical activity and exercise to relieve stress. Don't worry about your emotional state. I remember one evening after my swim when I picked up my order "to go" at the Boston Market. I saw two attractive women outside talking and laughing.

I realized I would have to walk by them to get to my truck. For some reason, I couldn't do it. I actually walked out the other door and around the building in order not to have them see me. Why did I take that much effort to avoid their glare? I really don't know, other than some nights I felt so lonely I could do nothing but deal with my loneliness, *alone.*

It all worked out; a new day came and I was up. I followed my routines, and went to the pool. I will not forget that alone time and how it really helped me to heal. Remember, re-singled means single. Rest and recovery means taking the time to reinvent yourself and blossom into a new identity. And routines are to build character, realizing doing something is usually better than doing nothing.

NINE

DIVORCE CLASS: IT'S GOING TO BE OKAY

I REMEMBER CLEARLY THE DAY I SAW the bulletin at the store where I would go every day to eat my lunch. It said, "Are you recently divorced? Having problems struggling with your emotions?" Those words spoke to me. I immediately called and left a message on the answering machine. The man offering the class, Adam, called me back within a few hours. We talked briefly. He said, "I'm having a class next Tuesday, would you like to come over?"

I asked him how many people would be there.

"Oh I don't know, maybe ten or twelve?"

I thought, "Great, not too many or too few." I was eagerly awaiting this new chapter in my life—Divorce Class. I had been divorced for about seven months; it was summer, and I was ready for a change.

Tuesday rolled around. I showed up at 7 p.m. sharp to greet my fellow divorcees. I noticed there were only two cars outside, Adam's and mine. I walked into his house. "Where is everybody?"

"It looks like it's just you and me," Adam replied.

I felt like walking out then and there. Perhaps I should have. Adam had been through two divorces—WOW! I could not imagine going through this twice. We talked and shared a few good stories. Adam appeared to be a nice enough person, but I soon realized he was more into helping himself than others. Apparently, he started these classes to hear himself talk. I did learn some things from him, but I wanted to attend a class where I could get input from more than one person. That was my first and last divorce class with Adam. The real class came three months later with a lot more in attendance.

THIS NEW CLASS happened to be at the old church where I attended when growing up. It was a Catholic class so I asked the instructor if I, no longer a Catholic, could attend.

"No problem, Mike; this class will help anyone."

This church helped me when I was going through a difficult time in high school, so I decided to try the class.

When I walked into that first class I honestly felt like I was the most screwed up person on earth. "I hope no one laughs at me; what will the women think? Will they judge me? I hope this class will help me." Somehow, I felt this was going to be a great learning experience.

The instructor, Jim, told everyone what to expect. "There will be eight sessions at two hours each." I was impressed; sixteen hours of this. I bet we will cover a lot of material.

There were twenty people in the class, eight men and twelve women, so I felt it might be a little biased. We sat around and Jim said, "Let's introduce ourselves and share our situation."

Mary started by saying she had been divorced for about a year and she hated her ex. She wished she had not gotten married.

Jim went next and said he had been divorced for

about three years and he was doing much better. (I suppose that's why they put him in charge.)

Kay said she had been divorced for about two years and had caught her husband having an affair. She went on to say when she found out and he was on his way back from the other woman's place, she tried to find the bullets to a gun so she could *shoot* him! She was serious, because I asked her.

Then Bill, looking down, shaking his head and pushing up his glasses stated, "I was married for thirty-five years and I'm having a real hard time." I commented: "Thirty-five years; that's a long time." He told us they fought a lot and had their share of problems, but he never thought he would be in his sixties and alone. I was really affected by Bill's comments.

Marilee, an Asian woman, said she was recently divorced and having a very difficult time. The tears began to well up in her eyes as she spoke of her children. She said, "I don't know what I'm going to do." Nevertheless, I noticed she was the *only* woman having a hard time. The rest were either apathetic or angry, while the men like Bill and me were sad. It was weird.

Marty spoke next. He was quiet and humble. He looked frightened and lonely. He merely stated that he did not know what to say.

I spoke last. "My name is Mike. I've been divorced for almost a year and my ex and I are still friends." I went on to say that, it ended at her request and I did not know why. I said, "We still live together."

All the women looked at me in total disbelief. "How could you live together? Did you have an affair? Did she? Do you still have sex?"

"No, that ended at the date of separation, as it should," I replied.

Why weren't they asking the other men these questions? Because they were not living with their ex-wives and I was. Actually, Bill said, he lived with his ex for about a year, to sell their house, which was the same reason I did it. Bill was old and wise but I was young. Almost all of the women felt I was foolish, especially Kay, the woman who tried to find the bullets to *kill* her ex.

That was about all the time we had in that first class. I realized something. Maybe I wasn't the most screwed up person in the class.

The second class: In this session, we talked about why each of our marriages failed and what we learned. Bill, Marty and I were the only men who did not have a cogent explanation as to why our marriages failed.

One man, Larry, was really pissed at his ex and said she left him for another man and she wanted sole custody of his children. "Can you imagine the nerve of that? I hate her, she's a real BITCH!" Everyone agreed. Jim, our instructor told Larry and all of us to "quit name-calling." We agreed. It's good advice. If you are in an intense argument, eliminate calling each other derogatory names. I know it sounds hard, but if you can start by doing that, you will recover faster.

I noticed many of the women used very harsh words when referring to their exes. I could see that most of them detested their former spouses. I asked myself, "Are these people faithful Christians?"

Everything considered this class was helping me. I could feel a big weight lifted as I went to each class. Most of the women said they did not know their husbands towards the end of their marriages because "he changed." Kay said this a lot until I finally asked, "Did he change or did you marry him knowing about his problems, but thought that you could fix him?"

"How dare you say that!" Kay retorted.

I heard that a lot throughout this class, and yes, I was proud of myself for asking that question.

Jim had some good points about the healing process.

One was to admit *you* were part of the marriage failure. Kay, who I affectionately called bullet woman, would not admit to this. Most of the women would not. But the men seemed okay with the idea.

One woman, Jane, kept saying, "Doesn't it seem all of us have been wronged in this?"

"I feel this a little, but I know I had something to do with my divorce because I married her," I said.

Jim smiled and agreed. He told everyone it's very Catholic to blame someone else, then go to confession and forget about it. I realized most of the women wanted the men to feel pity for them. After all, they were victims. I became the "victim" until I realized that if I played this card long enough, I would remain that way for the rest of my life. Don't we all play that card when we make a mistake and have too much pride to admit it? I was lucky to learn this priceless lesson early in my recovery.

One of Jim's good ideas—each week he would split the class up to crunch our feelings. Each group was supposed to be part women and part men.

ONE WEEK, BY the grace of God, I ended up in a group with all women. I admit I was intimidated. Jane said, "Oh, we got Mike with us, let's gang up on him."

Then they started to talk and ignore me. They were really going at it. One woman asked, "Where do you all go to meet guys?" Another woman responded, "I go to the Mountaineers Club." All of the women thought the men at that particular club were dorks. I spoke up, "Remind me not to go there." I was asked where I went to meet women. I replied, "*Not here!*" Actually, this got a good laugh and I started to feel less intimidated.

I went on, "I don't go anywhere to meet women because I don't feel as if I'm ready for a real relationship. I don't want to bring a woman into my miserable life right now." You should have seen their looks! Some of these "insensitive" women almost cried. They could not believe I, a man, had such emotions.

"Is that how you really feel?" Jane asked.

"Yes, it is." I was very emotional about my divorce and could not hide it. They started to look at me and talk to me differently when I indicated I was fearful of hurting a woman or being hurt by her. They began to realize I was a lot like them; human, with vulnerabilities.

I told them a story about a woman I had met after my separation, but before my divorce. Her name was May, and she taught me a lot. I met her at a park and started talking about my separation and struggles. She said she could tell I still loved my soon-to-be ex-wife. May had gone through a divorce about ten years before. She had to leave a mutually abusive relationship and admitted to having a temper and tendency towards violence. Her ex would hit her and say mean things and she acted the same way toward him; sometimes, for no other reason than jealousy.

She asked if my wife had a temper. I responded, "Not too much, other than pouring scalding coffee on me while riding with my boss in his truck, and throwing an old glass ashtray at my face." (The ashtray broke into three pieces when it hit me right between the eyes.)

Surprised, May said, "Oh my God, I bet that hurt!"

I told her about my own temper and how Connie and I had heated arguments that would last for hours.

Kay curiously asked why Connie poured the hot coffee on me. I said my boss, Tim, would pick me up in the morning and Connie would get a ride to her job as well. This was when we first lived together and neither of us had cars.

One morning we were driving along and Tim jokingly said, "Mike, do you want to see those girls again today? That one blond thought you were cute." Connie flared with jealous anger and poured the coffee on my face and neck. Tim said he was just kidding, but Connie was not listening. Tim pulled over; Connie got out and ran away. Her unwillingness to listen and jealous tirades were trademarks of her personality and behavior.

May advised me to be very careful going through my divorce. "What do you mean?" I asked curiously.

"I bet you want to go out and devour every woman you like."

I told her I didn't feel like that, because I was not right emotionally.

"But you will soon and when you do, be very careful." I told May I probably would have to get a rubber suit and some cans of Lysol before I started dating again.

May laughed and said, "That's not what I mean. I'm talking about 'bad karma.' You don't want other peoples' karma rubbing off on you, do you?" I didn't know if I believed in karma, but May had some good points. She said, "For every woman you sleep with, you carry some part of them with you for the rest of your life."

She went on to say, "If you go out there breaking hearts for fun, it will come back to haunt you."

"How could I break someone's heart when I myself have *no* heart to offer?" I asked.

May realized how much I still cared for Connie and

we eventually became friends because we understood each other.

All the women in the group wanted to know if I had slept with her, but I told them that wasn't important. The lesson I learned from May is, if a man plays with a woman's heart, eventually he will be burned. I felt vindicated because this was one thing on which all the women agreed with me. I bet everyone can remember when they first got their heart broken. That is your diploma for life. I know some men who cannot get over it.

That was my class with the women and I felt like I held my own. Some would talk to me after that, while others treated me with the same indifference they had before. That's okay; I have not tried to win any popularity contest in this life. I have found some women appreciate my honesty, while others despise me for it. My honesty is a reflection of my character. You will not start to heal unless you're honest about what happened in your marriage. That means telling the truth to yourself and others.

SOMETHING HAPPENED TO me when I was at the second class I will not forget. Remember Marty, the soft-spoken one, who said very little? At each class, we would take a break in the middle of the session. Marty and I were in the hallway looking into another class that seemed to be like a party.

"Look, Marty, they're having a great time in there."

"Yeah, looks like they're having fun."

"Who are they?" I asked.

"That's where you go when you finish our class," Marty said sadly.

I jokingly commented I couldn't wait to get to that class. Marty chuckled a little, "I don't know, Mike, sometimes I feel like throwing in the towel." I could tell by the look in his eyes he meant it. He looked crestfallen. I didn't know what to say so I kept quiet. We looked at those people laughing while we were crying on the inside.

I never saw Marty again after that class and I don't know what happened to him. I told the rest of the group what happened and they all felt bad. I wished I could have said something to help Marty. Jim advised, "You did the best thing for him Mike, you listened." I will not forget Marty and how he shared his feelings with me. I hope wherever he is he has found some comfort and peace.

I tried to watch what I said after that for fear of hurting anyone's feelings. That lasted until the seventh class when one woman told us about her annulment. Mary, the one who was pre-pissed all the time, said she was having her twenty-five-year marriage annulled.

I was curious, "What is that?"

Mary went on, "That's where you go before a priest and tell him and God your marriage was a mistake."

"Wait a minute; don't you have three kids with this man?" I asked.

"Yes I do."

"So when you say to God your marriage was a mistake, do you mean your kids are a mistake as well?"

Mary said this did not include the kids and she had to have the annulment in order to be remarried in the Catholic Church. I said, "You really believe that?" Another blank gaze came from Mary; unwilling to admit to her part of the failed marriage.

The Catholic Church does not condone divorce so you must have your marriage annulled. Then you can go tell your friends you were not married. The sperm used to create these kids came from heaven but not from your ex-husband. Wondering what the others thought, I paused for a minute, looked around the class and saw only blank faces. Did these people believe that? I asked Mary if she really believed that. She said, "Not really, but I'm going to do it."

"That has to be the stupidest thing I have ever heard

of," I responded. "You don't even believe in it, Mary."

She defended herself by saying she didn't care what I thought. "You may think it's stupid, but I believe it will work."

Before I replied, Jim spoke up, "Mike, will you please respect other peoples' beliefs?" I apologized to Mary and the rest of the class. Everyone is entitled to his or her beliefs.

Since that time, I became friends with a woman who also had an annulment many years ago. She is Catholic and confided with me she was married too young. Her husband was abusive and after only one year, told her goodbye. Realizing her mistake, she turned to annulment. In this instance, I fully understand her reasoning. However, Mary had been married for twenty-five years and had three children, so I felt her annulment was just an excuse to cover up her own mistake.

In spite of this, I felt better about my divorce and this class specifically. Jim had good ideas for recovery and I could tell he was doing well with his own. He had three years under his belt and I only ten months, so I could see that "Father Time" helps healing. Nevertheless, time alone is not enough; you must work at the healing process.

IT WAS MY last class and I was feeling proud. When I started this ordeal, I felt I had no options but misery. Upon finishing I realized there were real ways to cope with divorce. I have everyone in this class to thank for this. I sat through every minute of this divorce class, even when at times I did not feel like going.

Two comments were made to me in the last class that I still laugh about. Jim had everyone gather to share what he or she learned and to discuss our future plans.

I went first, "I can't believe how much I've learned from all you people."

"Oh really, Mike, what did you learn?" Mary teased.

"When I first walked into this class, I thought I was the most screwed up person in the world." That got everyone's attention. I continued, "But after eight weeks of this and hearing all these bizarre stories, I feel I am doing much better. I have no idea what to expect from the future, but I know for sure I will make it, even if that means spending the rest of my life alone."

Jane spoke, "You should spend a long time alone before you start dating."

Laughing inside, "Why is that Jane?" I asked.

With a pontificating look, she said, "I heard you need two years to recover for every one year you were married."

Okay, let's do the math. I was married fourteen years, times that by two and the grand total is twenty-eight. Therefore, Jane wanted me to wait twenty-eight years until I could date again. That would put me somewhere in my early sixties. I said, "Jane, what about you?" (I knew she was married for twenty-five years and had to be close to fifty) "So that almost puts you into triple digits before you're ready."

Jane, being Jane, responded, "Oh, no, I'm talking about you, not me." Jim and I looked at each other and smiled.

Remember Kay—the bullet woman? She went on to say that, she would *never* trust another man. I realized she would continue to clutch onto her anger. I stated, "I'm not that mad anymore but I am still very emotional." My anger had turned into sorrow. I told them I used to force myself into seclusion and could not envision re-marrying.

Kay's response: "Why not? Mike, you can always get another divorce."

I told her I had not thought of a marriage as disposable, like a piece of trash. That got a few laughs, but not from Kay.

It was obvious Kay couldn't be reached. And I no longer felt the need to try. Some people cannot be reached. I strongly recommend attending a divorce class. If you decide to go, don't be alarmed at what some people say or do. Divorce can do weird things to peoples' minds. Go to learn, cope, heal, understand and ultimately find closure.

We all said our goodbyes and I thanked Jim for helping me in so many ways. He invited me to the next class (Divorce Class—Part Two). Actually, we were all invited to the end of that class where we could talk to the graduates of Part Two. I sat down and realized I was not going to attend this class. I looked at those people and thought, "I don't need to hear any more rhetoric in order to recover." Perhaps it is best for some Catholics to attend repeatedly, until they figure it out.

What did I learn?

One: My failed marriage was at least half my fault and I had to accept that.

Two: Women look at marriage and divorce differently than men.

Three: I was going to make it! I was going to be okay. And, I felt a lot better about myself.

DRIVING HOME THAT night I experienced many emotions. What do I do now? Do I start dating? How do I approach myself as a re-singled man? I almost forgot we were supposed to call ourselves re-singled, NOT divorced. I thought that was silly then, but now it makes more sense.

It was almost a new year, 1998. I was listening to the radio and the song, *"In the Air Tonight,"* came on. I remembered how I felt when I first heard that song in 1981 and was moving out of my parents' house into an apartment with Connie. I felt like it was a new beginning and a new me. I remember hearing an interview with Phil Collins, and he was commenting on how he wrote that song after he went through a divorce. The irony was remarkable and I really did feel like I was *"Waiting for that moment for all of my life."*

TEN

DATING, GAME AND ADVICE

FROM MY EXPERIENCE I CAN TELL YOU that dating reflects the funniest, strangest, and at times, loneliest part of my life. Why? Looking back now it is easy to answer. The main reason was I was dealing with total strangers. There is a big difference between knowing a person and dating a person. Usually you date a stranger. Imagine how women feel; they risk going somewhere with a man that could be a serial killer. This creates a lot of stress for people who don't even know each other.

Let me confess I suck at dating. I really do. I have no patience for an art that men are supposed to master.

Maybe it's because I didn't date much before I got married. I had one girlfriend in high school, whom I met at a Catholic retreat. So all I did was ask her to see me again. Sure, I saw other girls, but that was mostly at social events and working at the Seattle Center, which was a great place to meet girls from all over the world.

I was a young, strong teenager, but had no game. I worked in the food service department for my dad. He expected me to work hard and make a name for myself. Some of the most memorable times in my life were while working for my dad at the Seattle Center.

If I saw a girl I liked, I would invite her to see me after work and go on any ride free, as I could get free passes. One problem, I worked the day shift because my mother didn't want me there at night. Seattle Center could be very dangerous at night. Also, my dad worked at night and if I asked a girl out, I would eventually run into him; I didn't want this. I had no car so I would have to catch a bus downtown. If I missed the last bus at 11:30 p.m., I would be stuck overnight in downtown Seattle, an even more dangerous place than the Seattle Center to be at night.

One day that I worked, I asked a girl if she wanted to go on some rides. She said, "Okay, but my friend has to come along." When I got off work at 6 p.m., I grabbed some ride passes, the girls, and proceeded to go have fun. They thought I was a king. They had free food, rides, and me to go with it. Not a bad deal I thought.

One ride I hated was called "The Roundup." This thing went round and round while slowly ascending and descending. The girls didn't like it either. As we walked by, the ride jockey challenged me to get on. Not wanting to back down in front of my new friends, I got on. I hadn't noticed it was getting late and I was the only one on the ride. John, the ride jockey decided to take *me* for a ride! Up and down and round and round for ten minutes. The only thing I noticed about the people on the ground is they were laughing at me. I wasn't laughing because I knew what was about to happen.

When I finally got off I spray-painted the pavement with my vomit and fell down in a delirious daze. The girls were not impressed and left me lying there. I guess someone rolling around in throw up was not very sexy to them. I thanked John for the ride and the embarrassment and went to catch the late bus covered in my own heave. I thanked God my father was not there to witness any of this. I felt I was destined to have bad luck in the dating world.

After my divorce I eventually started dating again. In 1998, I went on an astonishing twenty-two dates. To put that in perspective, this was more dates than I had been on in the previous twenty-two years. I was a babe in the woods, even though I wasn't exactly a kid at thirty-six.

INTERNET DATING

MY SECOND DATE in 1998 was with a girl I "met" online. It was a strange ride. I used to go into chat rooms occasionally and meet new people. I liked a New Zealand chat room because I figured I would be completely anonymous there. I would talk about what was happening in the Seattle area.

One night the chat room leader noticed I was talking to a girl from the Seattle area. He said, "Hey, Sandy, it looks like Mike is from your area." Actually, she was from Port Townsend, which is about two hours away from my location, Duvall, Washington. Sandy and I exchanged phone numbers and started talking over the phone. She was also recently divorced, so I felt we had a lot in common. Sandy was ten years younger and had a child. Everything seemed normal. I soon found out in meeting strangers, people are not always what they seem.

We met on a Friday. I drove and caught the ferry to Port Townsend. There was a catch—Sandy wanted to bring along a friend, since we were meeting for the first time. I reluctantly agreed because I wanted her to feel as comfortable as possible. Sandy assured me her friend would not be a third wheel, and we would have plenty of time to be alone. That was where the lies started.

It is very easy to catch a stranger in lies. I bought Sandy and her friend, Debbie, dinner. We talked, ate and started having a good time. They were nice, so I relaxed. Debbie, Sandy's friend, suggested we go out for a few drinks.

"Come on, Mike, we'll treat."

I'm not much of a drinker, especially when it comes to hard liquor. I made it a point to take it slow. But Sandy and Debbie were really pounding them down. Then the lies started to unfold. Every time Sandy went to the bathroom, Debbie would tell me something about Sandy I did not know. Remember, Sandy said she was divorced and I had no reason to doubt her. Sandy always had her hands folded and I was starting to wonder why.

The drinks flowed as the night progressed. Both women were getting a buzz on. They drank three drinks to my one and it showed on their faces. Sandy finally unfolded her hands; I saw an impressive diamond ring. She went to the bathroom and Debbie told me that Sandy was still married. I exclaimed, "I saw that huge ring!" Debbie said Sandy had frantically been trying to remove it before we met, which explained her folded hands. Sandy kept trying to get it off in the bathroom.

Becoming honest, Debbie said she was also married and was there to cheat on her husband. She said that right to my face, as if she was interested in me. Even if she were not married, Debbie would definitely be one of the most undesirable women I have ever met.

After that, I was seriously looking for an exit, just to get away from these *freaks*. How in the hell did I walk into this? I felt stupid. What if their husbands walked in and saw us having drinks? We were in a small town with no escape and the last ferry had already left. Men are shot for things like this. There is nothing worse than a jealous husband. So I made up my mind to leave, but I had to wait for the opportunity. They became blissfully drunk and I suggested going elsewhere. We walked along the waterfront and there was a boat that was playing loud hard rock music. I told them I would get on that boat.

"You can't get on that boat, Mike, so quit bragging."

Actually, I wanted *them* on that boat and far away from me. We followed it as it docked and some evil-sounding punk band played angry music. I thought these girls belonged on this boat.

We boarded and they started to dance satanically to the rhythm of ominous noise. Everyone on this boat was dancing to the music but me. They seemed to be in a trance, uncontrollably moving their bodies like puppets. I felt an overwhelming need to get off that boat. I saw my chance right before we left port, and jumped ship. Only a six-foot jump, but Carl Lewis would have been proud because my adrenaline was flowing and it was the right thing to do. Elated, I went back to my hotel room and went to bed—alone.

From the vantage point of my hotel room, I could see and hear that boat moving slowly back and forth in the harbor through most of the night. What a perfect fit, two evil girls on one evil boat. I was up to leave early the next morning and the desk clerk told me, "Hey, your friends got back here at 4 a.m."

"They're not my friends," I proudly replied.

Driving home, I said to myself, "What an idiot. I can't believe I fell into their trap."

So, if you are considering internet dating, be careful. You can find yourself in a very dangerous situation. The internet can be a good place to meet people and have fun. At the same time, it can also be a place where deceitful people lie and play games.

Despite what happened I didn't give up. I did realize after this experience, I would have to be much more cautious. Sandy was dishonest from the very beginning, and it was only a matter of time before I found out. She e-mailed me later, but I told her the next time she went out pretending to be divorced it might be a good idea to lose that huge rock on her finger. She said she was sorry, and I said goodbye.

NINETEEN NINETY-EIGHT WAS a very strange year. I learned about women and myself. I learned there are many lonely people out there, some even lonelier than I was. When the lonely gravitate toward one another, surprising things can happen.

I met another girl online named Julie. I took her to

dinner and a movie, when for some unknown reason; she walked away without even saying goodbye. She called a few days later and wanted to see me again.

"Wait a minute; first tell me why you walked away after the movie."

"You made me nervous and I didn't know what to say or do, so I just walked away," Julie responded.

We met again and I noticed this time how good she looked. She had shiny dark red hair with a warm smile. We talked in her car for hours then I said, "Goodnight." I wanted to kiss her but wasn't sure if she did.

About a week later, Julie called in a frantic voice, "Mike, can I talk to you?"

"Are you okay?" I asked.

She started crying and said she had taken ten tablets of her medication when she was only supposed to take two.

"My God, Why did you do that?"

She said she didn't want to feel any more pain that day. Julie had a problem with her leg. I noticed a cane in her car but she seldom used it.

"Julie, check yourself into the hospital right away, you've overdosed," I urged her.

"Sometimes I take too many pills for my pain." She seemed to recover and settled down. I felt my talking to her was helping.

Then she told me a strange story. She said one time she took fifteen of these pills. I don't know what they were and I don't care because I hate pills that mess with your mind and body. Anyway, she said she took the pills and fell asleep. When she awoke, there was an ambulance outside her house. From her sliding glass door, she noticed medics pulling a sheet over a body. She went outside to see who died. The girl was Julie—herself.

I told her this premonition was her brain telling her to stop! Please stop! She agreed, but said that sometimes she just could not stand the pain. I said her premonition would eventually come true one day if she continued taking too many pills. She seemed okay afterwards and maybe I scared her into soberness. I only talked with her one time later and she barely remembered what happened. People who take narcotics excessively, or "do drugs," seem to have little sense of time.

On and on I went, date after date. I got my heart broken, my feelings hurt, and my wallet *drained*. Yes, gentlemen, you had better be ready to shell out some cash when you start dating. Women say they want equal rights, except when it comes to who asks whom out and who will pay for the date. Those unglamorous jobs are reserved for men.

GET SOME GAME DUDE:
HOW WOMEN REALLY SEE YOU

IT'S TIME TO go to a mirror and take a good long look at *you*. What do you see? Maybe you see a little of Tom Cruise and Brad Pitt. Too bad women do not see you that way. I realize how most women see me and I have no problem with it; I learned long ago I am good enough. Call it confidence, or cockiness, it *doesn't* matter; all I know is I do have some game. When a woman says this, it's considered sexy; when a man does, it's considered arrogant. In short: *There is no such thing as "equal rights" in dating.*

Go out and buy some nice clothes. Start with a pair of slacks and a fine dress shirt; do not forget shoes. Women love nice shoes. Just look around their closets and you will see twenty pairs of shoes for every pair in a man's closet.

Next, look at your grooming. Do you keep clean? I swim almost every day and shower four times. (When I do, I have to shower before and after each swim.) If I am going out for the evening, I shower again, because I don't want the smell of chlorine on me. Get yourself groomed, showered, shaved and clean. Women do not like a man who smells bad. And please lay off the aftershave; most women do not want to smell some cheap bottle of cologne on a man.

What about the car you drive? Women love cool cars for the same reasons men do; they look sexy in them. If she likes you and feels sexy in your car, good things will happen.

Yet women like different things for completely different reasons. Why? Who knows? It is one of life's mysteries. I have learned if you try some stupid pickup line, you will be rejected no matter how good you look. Simply walk up to her, look her in the eye and say, "Hello, how are you?" You will be surprised by her response.

Try a little tenderness. Remember, women like soft things: soft music, soft pillows, and soft laughter. No matter what anyone says, bringing her flowers never gets old. Smile at a woman you like or she will not know you're interested. If she is not interested and you keep pursuing her, you're a *jerk*. Guys, it is time to walk away. Remember, there are over *three billion* women on this earth. You can muster up enough game to get at least *one*.

Don't try to be something you are not. Be what you are, a well-dressed confident man who has direction and purpose. Almost all women think that is very sexy.

BE AWARE OF ADVICE

ISN'T IT AMAZING how the people who often have no idea what they are talking about offer the most advice? I remember a happy, content, married woman who presented me with her advice. She was an acquaintance, not a friend. She told me she had a friend for me to go out with, but she wanted me to wait to call her. I said, "Wait for what?" This woman was also an acquaintance of Connie's and said she didn't want to disrespect my wife by setting me up with another woman. "You mean 'ex-wife,'" I said. Almost all the women I knew at that time were still calling Connie my wife, even though our marriage had been over for almost a year. It was strange.

This happily married woman went on about how I should just wait, go home, and wait.

"How long do you think I should do that?"

Her comeback, "I think you need to be alone right now." This meant I would not be meeting her friend for a date. All this advice was coming from someone who had a warm body to sleep with every night.

This was advice from someone who had no idea, or has forgotten what it's like to be *alone*. Even if she were in an unhealthy relationship, she still would not have an idea what it's like to come home to an empty house, knowing you will go to bed and wake up by your-self.

When you're re-singled, people who are married have no conception of what you're going through. Don't waste your time listening to their advice on dating. Talk to other men and women who are going through the same situation; they can relate to your position. Don't ever try to take someone else's grief away. The best thing to say when you don't know what to say is, "I'm sorry." By listening to someone and not judging them or telling them what to do, you allow them to voice their feelings. In doing so you establish trust and let that person know it's going to be okay. We all need someone who will listen.

ELEVEN

THOSE LOST SOULS

HAVE YOU EVER KNOWN A LOST SOUL? A few years ago a woman with a low, raspy voice called me out to her house to do some landscape reclamation. Over the phone, she sounded older and weak, so I figured she was an older woman who needed some good old American muscle. When I arrived and saw her face to face, I thought, "Is this the same lady I talked with over the phone?" She admitted she had a cold and her voice was a little hoarse. I remember looking into her eyes and thinking, "This woman looks lost."

She was attractive and looked a lot younger than I expected. Her name was Sheri. We talked about her house and what she wanted me to do. This was a cool house. It overlooked the local winery and Woodinville Valley. There were stables for horses and one of them was the grandson of none other than our local legend, "Seattle Slew." You could tell by looking at this horse it was from champion stock.

Sheri could sense I was fascinated with that horse and asked me if I wanted to ride him. "Not today; maybe someday." I am a little scared of horses because of something that happened to me when I was younger. I stayed a long time and Sheri commented on how much she enjoyed talking with me. But, this was a business visit, so I asked why she called me out? I gave her a bid and then told her to think about it. She said, "Oh, go and do it, I'm sure you'll do a good job." Sheri was friendly and I left there thinking something might happen between us.

I proceeded to get right to work on her house. I wanted to do a good job as always. It's my business and I'm very particular about my work. We cleaned everything up and put some new bark down, achieving landscape reclamation.

One funny thing happened when we were blowing

bark in the pouring rain. That ornery horse kept looking at me, so I said to my worker, "Watch, this will put a scare in him." I pointed the bark hose in front of him, spewing bark out with an incredible force, but this horse stood there like a statue, imposing and unaffected by my challenge. The grandson of Seattle Slew remembered my prank later when I finally did ride him and he pushed me into a wood rail.

I finished the job and Sheri was pleased with my work. I thought that was the end of our relationship because I didn't feel comfortable about asking her out, even though I truly wanted to.

It came time for payment. Rather than send a check, she asked if I was going to be in the area to pick it up. Coincidentally, I was going on a date with a girl I had known for a while. We had arranged to have dinner at a nice restaurant near Sheri's house. I always dress nicely when going to this restaurant. I asked my date if I could drop by and pick up the check. "No problem, but hurry, I'm hungry."

When I walked into her house, Sheri had company. "You look very nice, Michael, where are you going?" she asked.

Sensing her interest, "Out to dinner with a friend."

She had only seen me in my work clothes before, so it must have been a surprise for her to see me dressed up. Sheri's friends wanted to know who I was and if we had something going on. Later Sheri told me she wished I were taking her out that night. I told her I felt the same way. I took the check from her and figured it would be the last time I saw her.

ABOUT A WEEK later, Sheri called me. She said she really liked my work and would refer me to her friends. We talked, laughed and I could tell she wanted more. I took a chance and asked if she wanted to go out sometime.

"I was going to ask you the same thing," she responded.

I felt she was telling the truth, but couldn't say the words. I also broke a longstanding rule, "Never get involved with any customers." Oh well, I suppose the side of me that loves to break rules, did. I knew if a relationship didn't work out I could be assured I would not get that customer back. I stuck to the "no involvement rule," until I met Sheri.

WE WENT OUT and had a great time. Sheri loved to stay up late, talk, and carry on. She had a huge circle of friends who would wait to spend time with her. I told her I thought that was silly. I would not wait around for the privilege of spending time with someone. Curious, she asked why. I told her I don't compete for any woman's time. If she wants to spend time with me, then she will. I told her there is no bigger turn off to me than a woman who does not reciprocate.

So in the beginning, she found time for me and we did everything together. We went out to dinner, movies, hiking, for walks and out for drives. She had a special edition Jaguar. This car had 12 cylinders of pure power and Sheri let me drive it anytime I wanted. Our affair took off like a rocket, but like some of the early NASA rockets, we crashed and burned. But not before I fell in love with this strange and mysterious lost soul.

Sheri would talk about how she was married for years and devoted to her husband. She mentioned when she was dating, she did not fall in love. In fact, she said she had never been in love. I immediately interrupted and said; "You were married for twelve years to someone you did not love?" She evaded my question and spoke about how she stayed faithful. Cornering her, I asked, "Did you love him or not?" She confessed she didn't and married him thinking she would eventually fall in love, but never did. I told her that was pathetic and how I was totally in love when I got married and would not consider marrying someone I did not love.

We talked a lot about love and relationships. I even told her about Karla, how I loved her at such a young age. Sheri said, "You were a baby and had no idea what you were doing." I said she sounded jealous.

I told her the story about my first true teenage love—Karen. Sheri still seemed to think I was too young to understand the concept of love. She asked me, "Okay, Michael, how did you know you loved her?" I knew I loved Karen when I looked in her eyes, and she in mine, and seeing each other's reflection—understanding completely how we felt. I did tell Karen I loved her many times. I described how those special times when a "look" from her said more than words could express.

Sheri refused to talk about love anymore. I could not understand how Sheri had not been in love her entire life. She was almost forty and did not know what it felt like. This bothered me, especially in the beginning of our relationship; but by the end, it made perfect sense.

Sheri had intimacy issues in every way possible. She would make up any excuse not to get close or intimate with me. On the rare occasions we had sex, I felt like the only willing participant. I came to realize this was not going to change and Sheri was a "lost soul" I could not reach. It was difficult to understand why she had intimacy issues, but after being shot down so many times for even mentioning love, I was beginning to lose interest.

I believe the worst feeling in the world is to love someone and not have them love you in return. Such was our relationship. It's not that she didn't care, but I wanted—I mean really *wanted*—this woman to love me, but it did not happen.

I remember her saying, "Don't say you love me. If you do, don't expect much in return."

Can you imagine my humiliation? Did this woman have no soul—or understanding of love at all? I knew it was just a matter of time before my relationship with Sheri would end.

IT WAS MY 42nd birthday, July 3, 2003. Sheri came to my house and picked me up for dinner and some fun. She looked great and let me drive that awesome car. We went out to dinner and then sped around in the "Jag." Returning to my place, she actually stayed until 4 a.m., the latest she ever stayed over. I went for a walk after she left, on the birthday of my country. I saw the day come alive with the sunrise and said, "Life is good." I had a great birthday and will always be thankful to Sheri for that. This was the last good time we had together.

ABOUT A MONTH later, after a dance class that happened to be close to Sheri's house, I stopped by to say hello. She seemed distant and not very nice. I could tell things were different, a feeling that happens when relationships fall apart. I sat down on her couch and we talked. Sheri said she was ready to spend more time with me, which I thought was interesting since I had done everything I could to spend time with her. I had lost interest in this lost soul.

We talked back and forth. I told her no matter how each of us saw our relationship, it was not going to work. She grew more frustrated and I could see this was going nowhere. Upset, Sheri picked up her remote and began to channel surf like a game day maniac. This made me furious because she did this once before and I vowed that if it ever happened again, I would walk out.

"Could you please stop doing that?" I asked her nicely.

She returned a glazed look. Melancholy from her indifference, I waited awhile and thought about what I had promised myself before. I stood up and started walking toward the door. That got her attention and the TV was not important to her now, but it was too late. I was done; completely finished with this one-sided relationship.

I cannot explain how hard it was to walk away from this woman. I knew this decision was going to hurt me more than her. It was something I had to do. As I was leaving, she suddenly paid attention to me. I knew she could feel finality in my footsteps. She came toward me as I was moving to my truck. "You're just going to leave like this?"

I looked at her and said, "Yes, it's time. Goodbye."

When I arrived home there was a message on my landline from Sheri saying, "How rude for you to walk out on me like that." I immediately called back wanting to explain why I walked away, yet only got her answering machine. I left her a message saying if she wanted to know the real reason why I left, she could call and I would explain it to her. I never heard her voice again.

Sheri did send me a few cards and I stopped by her house after receiving a Christmas card one year; but she was having a party and I did not want to barge in unannounced.

It was almost Christmas 2004; I went there with my

card and flowers (Sheri has a birthday right before Christmas.)

As I was driving over, I thought about explaining what happened and why I left that night. I felt she would want closure to our relationship. I was wrong.

When I arrived, there were cars everywhere, no place to park. I drove around the block a few times. On that last loop, I saw Sheri standing in the window. She was entertaining guests, wearing a white sweater, and looking happy. She couldn't see me, but I could sure see her. I sat and stared until I got depressed, and drove away.

When I saw a friend of hers heading toward the house, I asked this friend if she would give Sheri the card and flowers.

"No problem."

I explained in the card if she wanted to talk, she could call me. I did not hear from Sheri again.

It has been a long time since I last saw Sheri. I think about why I let myself fall in love with this woman. I compare my relationship with Sheri to walking into a room full of strangers. The people in the room all know each other, but not one of them knows you. At first, everyone seems friendly and you try to fit in. Then you realize their friendliness is a façade. Walking into that room was your first mistake, closing the door was the second, and sticking around trying to fit in (or in my case waiting for Sheri to love me) was the third. I made all three mistakes with Sheri. It took some time to recover and I still wonder about her.

That relationship had a profound effect on me. From then on, I was very careful about with whom I chose to be involved. Sheri made me realize the importance of a healthy reciprocal relationship. I cannot thank her enough. When I was walking away from her I knew in my heart, it was the last time. I would walk away from her a million times, because this is the right thing to do. Sheri wanted me to love her without loving me in return. I do feel bad for her and hope one day she will understand *love*. Sometimes, it is best to wish someone well—and let them go.

People with intimacy issues are very unpredictable. It is often difficult to detect this in someone, even if you think you know the person. Understand you are taking a huge risk if you fall in love with someone like that. It's better to be upfront and honest about your issues, whatever they might be. This will save a lot of time and heartache. After Sheri, I did a serious reevaluation and searched deep within myself.

However, I did not then, nor will I ever, give up on love. If I do, I will be like Sheri—unreachable and another lost soul.

TWELVE

A MAN'S FEELINGS

AN OLD BOB SEGER SONG GOES: *"Until you've been beside a man, you don't know how he feels."*
Isn't that true? I remember one time talking with a woman, unaware of my feelings, when she said, "I can just tell how you feel by the look on your face."

"That's amazing; I wasn't even aware how I feel." The conversation about my feelings ended.

We are all guilty of this. We often assume how someone is feeling, or what he or she is thinking, when in actuality, we don't know. I suppose that is human nature, but it's based upon a false premise. It is ridiculous to believe one can actually know how another person feels.

It is true; women are more in touch with their feelings than men are. They confide in each other while men often do not. But that doesn't mean a woman is more in touch with a man's feelings. Their mothering nature yearns to calm us down and make everything okay. Women are correct in their application of talking about their feelings and sharing problems with each other.

Men say things like: "Suck it up, walk it off, buck up, deal with it, or the old standard: take it like a man." My personal favorite is "*Get over it!*" Ironically, eventually that is what we may need to do. Those old sayings are tired and worn out. Guys, accept your emotions, and learn to process them. It's okay to talk to others about your feelings.

Being a man doesn't come with an instruction booklet. The women I have known understand I am a deep-feeling and sensitive person. I acquired that trait from my father and it is something I am proud of. My father's character was revealed when we lived in the Greenwood area of Seattle.

. . .

WE KIDS USED to love to go to Herfy's restaurant and devour as much food as we could consume. One hot summer day, we were there having fun when I noticed a man
eating individual packets of ketchup and mustard. He
had a beard, mustache, and long hair in a ponytail. It
was the first time I ever saw a man with hair like that.
Before long, the entire family was around him asking
questions. My father asked him, "When was the last time
you had a meal?"

He responded in a very low tone, "I haven't eaten for
three days."

No wonder he was eating those packets! I wanted to
help him. I could not imagine having no food for three
days. I was looking at my father saying to myself, "Please
help this man." This man liked the attention. He went on
about all the cities he had been to and how he loved to
travel, "seeing the sights." I felt a strong affection toward
this humble soft-spoken stranger. My father asked,
"Where will you sleep tonight?" The pony-tailed man said
he did not know, but his destination was Canada.

We were all looking at this man and at my father, and
wondering what my dad would do. My dad reached
into his wallet, took out a dollar bill, and handed it to the

man under the table. We saw what happened but no one else in the restaurant did. Our new friend instantly went to order as much food as he could consume with that dollar. This was in 1970 when you could get a good meal for a dollar. I don't think I ever saw a man eat like that. While he was eating his meal, we talked and laughed and for a little while, I believe he felt like he was part of our family. Then it came time to say goodbye. My dad wished him good luck and this stranger thanked him for his generosity and kindness.

We all crammed into the Plymouth station wagon and I was in the very back seat facing the back window. I kept looking at the restaurant and wondering about my new friend. I asked my dad, "Where will he go? Where will he sleep? How will he buy food with no money?"

"He'll be okay son; that's the life he's chosen; some day you'll understand."

I started crying, realizing I would never see this stranger again.

IT HAS BEEN over five years since my father died and I still think about what he did that day. I now understand completely the gesture of kindness he gave a total stranger. It wasn't the money he gave him; it was the *way* he gave it to him—passing it under the table so no one else could see it. In this way, my father not only provided food to a man who was desperately hungry, but also preserved his dignity. Although it was only one dollar, my father showed me at a young age how to treat "a man's feelings." In all my years since that day at the restaurant, I have never witnessed such an act of kindness. God bless you Dad and thanks for the great lesson.

How DO WE process our feelings when facing a crisis? As I stated earlier, sometimes it is best to get some professional counseling. This is one time you need to buck up and do the right thing. Remember, divorce can foster devastating emotions. It can be overwhelming to travel the road of divorce and recovery—*alone.*

You don't have to be alone. You can occupy your time by going to a divorce class, talking to a friend, or offering help to someone else in need. Anything that will help you move on is a welcome benefit. I found understanding and acceptance by talking to others who went through divorce about our mutual calamity. Once you realize you're not alone, you won't feel so lonely.

I believe that new emotions are born from "the process." When men go through crisis and tragedy, unfamiliar feelings are summoned and our character is redefined. When we meet these challenges head on and accept the changes we must go through, we discover one more characteristic, integrity.

I found it very therapeutic to keep a journal. In high school, I used to take a class called, "Encounter." In that class, our teacher had us write in a journal every day. When I was going through my separation and divorce I started my journal writing again. Sometimes I go back and look at my innermost thoughts during the biggest challenge of my life. Writing in my journal helped me recover. It also made me realize "a man's feelings" are distinctively his own.

THIRTEEN

JUNE 10TH: THE WORST AND BEST DAY

THE DAY CONNIE CAME TO ME WITH THE NEWS that she wanted a divorce, June 10, 1996, became known as the DOS, or date of separation. Why am I bringing it up again? Because that was the worst day of my life up to that point and I want to explain how it became the *best* day.

Fast forward to June 10, 2006, it was a Saturday, I had worked a long week and I really did not feel like going out. Previously I had signed up to attend a singles dance party, but was having second thoughts about going. You show up at these things and walk around with a nametag that says, not so much your name, but you are desperate. I was not desperate that night, but I was certainly alone. I was perfectly aware of what day it was; it had been ten years since my marriage ended. I felt I had nothing to lose by showing up at this party.

The party was in Seattle, not too far from where I was born, so it was nice to get over to the big city and do some salsa dancing. I had been taking lessons for a while, knew a few moves, and wanted to show off my "Rico Sauvé."

I arrived early. The girl who ran the show immediately took my money and told me to fill out my nametag. I attended one other party she ran and thought she was rude by the way she was counting money in front of everyone. Her name is Mildred and before she could give me a grand tour, I simply walked away and went into the kitchen. In open defiance, I folded that nametag and put it in my pocket. If a girl wanted to know my name, she could find out the old-fashioned way: *ask.*

The crowd started to roll in and before long, Mildred, our singles leader, had all the men spend five minutes at each table. Each table had about two to three women and the men rotated around: Table speed dating on the ten-year anniversary of the worst day in my life.

At the first table, I met a man named Melvin. He was a well-dressed, good-looking black man and a real charmer. Most of the men there were geeks, sitting around looking nerdy. The first girl we spoke with was cute and had glitter all over her face. She told Melvin and me we were the only good-looking guys there. We were both flattered, but she seemed to like Melvin more. When the rotate bell went off, I rushed to the next table.

Table two featured a girl who just stared at me and laughed every time I said something. At first, I thought this was nice, but near the end, I wasn't sure if she was laughing at my jokes, or me.

Ding, ding—the next table. I was there with a few guys; one of whom was named Lou kept rambling, sweating and looking nervous. I asked, "Are you okay, Lou?" Sweating more, he replied, "Yeah, I'm fine." I asked the others if they had been to any of these parties before. It turned out they were members of Mildred's singles club. They paid a lot of money to join for the privilege to sit around and be rejected by these women. Some of the women were also members but they didn't pay much for membership. I was wondering if this party was a mistake.

Next, we had a dance session where two teachers showed everyone a dance move and then we would try it. I was ready to get out on the floor. The sun was setting and the entire room was filled with a golden wall of light. I felt better and I started to dance and have fun. This place was home to a dance club. Dancers started to show up and demonstrate their moves. I remember one old guy who knew every dance and all the moves. He danced with every available partner. Watching, I said to myself, "God bless America."

While I was waiting for my chance to salsa dance, I ended up hanging out with a girl named Lori. We had some things in common, but I was starting to think about leaving. I had done what I promised to do, not sit at home and feel sorry for myself on this historic day. I felt I would be better off letting the other men share the spoils.

I decided to walk into the kitchen for one last drink and hit the road. On my way in, I noticed a petite, attractive Asian girl leaning against the wall. She was wearing an impressive red dress with a white sweater wrapped around her neck. I approached her as if I was being pulled toward something but not understanding why. I smiled at her as I held out my hand in greeting. She lifted her hand slowly and I held it softly. "Hi, my name is Michael." When I touched this girl's hand, I realized this was no longer going to be just another night. When our hands met, and I looked into her dark brown eyes, I felt a profound sensation.

I wanted to be near her and the thought of leaving seemed ridiculous. I told her I was going into the kitchen to get water and asked if she would wait because I wanted to talk with her. When I returned, guess who had taken my place? Melvin! He was standing right where I was. Instead of interrupting them, I went to an open table and sat down.

Lori soon joined me and I could not help but look over at them to see if she was looking for me. She did look over at me and I felt like a little boy who had just lost his ball. Melvin had been doing this all night. After I was through talking to a girl, Melvin would approach her and talk longer. I saw him jot down a few phone numbers and was weary of him following me around. Besides there was no way he was going to get my girl.

I waited for my opening and got right back to this mysterious, charming young woman. We talked about many things and I wondered if she had any idea the impression she had on me. We danced and she looked so cute moving around the floor. I lost track of time, it started to get dark and I knew there would be a full moon soon. The full moon always has a powerful effect on my feelings.

She said her name was Bing and she was from Beijing, China, which was as far away from my birthplace, Seattle, as you can get. I wanted so badly to take her out of there and go for a walk in the moonlight, but I was still a stranger and I did not want to scare her away.

We talked about her parents. Her father had recently passed away and I told her my dad passed away four years ago, and how I still think about him every day. It was strange when I talked about my dad; I felt he was still around. I told her about my mother, that she lived alone and was in poor health. It was amazing how fast I fell for this girl, but that happens when the timing is right. I was having fun and didn't care about going home. I wanted to spend every minute with this girl from so far away.

If you know anything about my luck, you realize things never go smoothly for me. We walked into the kitchen. Mildred and Bing began talking. I noticed Mildred's scouring glare because I was not a paying member to her singles club, for I had told her she wanted way too much money. I sidestepped the situation and told Bing we would get caught up later. That was a huge mistake.

I started to talk to Lori again. Before you know it, she said she wanted to leave, so I offered to walk her to her car. This was near downtown Seattle and it was dark, so I was trying to do the right thing. Lori said I was a gentleman. When we arrived at her car, there was a note under her windshield wiper, so I knew she had other admirers. I said goodbye and like a homing pigeon, I headed back to the dance hall.

I looked around, but didn't see my little China girl. Did she leave? Not another Karla situation. I returned to the kitchen and she was standing exactly where I left her but she was talking with Melvin. My blood began to boil! I wanted to walk up to that guy and tell him to get away from *my* girl. But of course, I didn't do that, and I hoped Bing did not see the glare of rage and disappointment on my face. This was enough for me. I walked out feeling defeated.

As I DROVE home, I felt emotional havoc. I wanted to feel sorry for myself, but I couldn't. Instead, I thanked God for that night and how glad I was to meet Bing. I was fortunate for having the courage to get out of my house instead of moping around. I was satisfied to know that even though our time together was short, I was happy to have met her. I would not forget Bing and how I felt when our hands touched.

I did have the presence of mind to give her my phone number. If she wanted to call me, she could. As I drove across the I-90 Bridge, I saw that huge moon reflecting on the majestic water of Lake Washington. I thought, "I wish she would call." The pull of the moon exposed my loneliness. I felt strange thinking about what just happened and how I already missed her. I looked at the moon one more time and wondered if I would ever see this girl again.

Then, my cell phone rang. I sensed it might be her but didn't know what to say. It was Bing! I said I was glad she called. She told me she looked at my face when I came back and saw the fury in my eyes. I was hoping she did not see me. I started to calm down and asked her if I could see her again, without all the commotion. Bing told me she felt bad not being able to say goodbye at the party. That said a lot about her character and integrity. Finally I did something right and knew deep down going to that party was my destiny.

TEN YEARS! THAT is a long time. I have never waited around for the right girl to come along. I always felt like that would be foolish. Yes, there were times when I was unbelievably lonely, but always felt there was someone for me. Neither Bing nor I wanted to go to that dance, but we did.

You will not meet any girl waiting at home feeling sorry for yourself. You have to get out there and take your chances. You might be hurt, disappointed and let down, or you might meet someone special. My spirit was so low, at times; I honestly thought my only option was to be alone. Isolating yourself is not a good idea.

I don't feel that way anymore. In the worst of times, I still thanked God for my life. I realized if I kept trying, I would eventually find someone for me. I did not anticipate meeting someone like Bing on the ten-year anniversary of my separation. The paradoxical quirk of fate is incredible. It is enough to transform June 10th, the worst day, into the best day.

FOURTEEN

MY CHINA GIRL

I HAVE TO DEVOTE A CHAPTER TO MY DEAREST BING, for it was she who inspired and encouraged me to write this book. If you ever saw her, you would never forget her. She may be small in stature but whatever she lacks in size, she makes up for in integrity.

Bing has straight black hair and dark brown eyes. That's the first thing I noticed about her, those eyes, and how she looked into the core of my being. When I touched her hand the night we met, I sensed pain and emotion. Bing had suffered a lot in her life, but I have not heard her complain. From listening to me this long, it is safe to say no one would say that about me. We are different and at the same time so much alike. So many people fight about their differences and don't take the time to really know each other. We didn't start out that way. We listened to one another and had many deep conversations over the phone. We wanted to know and understand each other.

I remember Bing telling me how she first lost her mother, then her cat, followed by her father, all within a nine-month period. To make matters worse, she did not have the opportunity to return to China, where her parents lived and died, to say goodbye. The look in her eyes as she told me this, defined sorrow and reminded me of how I felt when I lost my father and more recently, my mother. But I had the chance to say goodbye.

Bing went on to say that after her mother died, she kept walking around her apartment area in the rain with a dark red umbrella. Since she told that story, I have imagined running into her and how I wished I could have helped. But of course, she had to grieve and cope alone. All those times alone helped us to appreciate each other. Bing and I in no way take each other for granted.

SHE HAD SHARED this story one night when we were at the base of Snoqualmie Falls. We had just met two weeks earlier and I told her I wanted to take her somewhere special. We parked at the bottom and walked to the overlook area. First, you must make that walk, some of which is in total darkness. She stopped a few times saying, "It's too dark; I don't want to go down there."

"Just trust me and hold my hand. I'll take care of you," as I tried to comfort her.

After about ten stops, and much trepidation, we finally arrived at a spot you must see to appreciate—glorious Snoqualmie Falls. There, Bing told me her story and we became special friends. As the waterfall crashed in front of us, she confided in me her sorrow. She cried, and as I held her, I felt her small powerful heart beat and realized I would *always* love this woman. We held each other as the waterfall soothed our souls. I forgot about the pain in my heart. I have not felt alone since that night.

My little China girl can see right through me. She is the equivalent of a walking scanner, always observing and evaluating every situation. When she moves her eyes from left to right quickly, you can be certain she is paying close attention to everything. If you are not accurate about what you say or do, she will draw it to your attention and ask why you said one thing and did another.

She balances me and calms me down when I most need it. She says I do the same for her, and when I hear that, I relax and realize things will be okay. I will be okay.

It has been over a year since we met. Our relationship has grown and our love for each other blossomed. We have made plans to marry and start a new life together. Bing made me realize it is okay to love and trust someone again. Our love for each other has enabled me to move on. When I am with her, it just "feels right." Thanks for being there for me, Sweetie, and I will always love you.

FIFTEEN

EMBRACE THE NEW YOU EVERY DAY

I F YOU'RE RECENTLY DIVORCED, I hope this book has given you some real ways to heal. Eventually the pain will ease and the new you will emerge. When that happens, feel fortunate and thank God, or whatever your higher power may be. Congratulations, you survived. Yet, it is not about embracing the new you today; it is about embracing the new you *every day*. You will go through constant changes and struggles and you must be malleable and willing to adapt. If you are not flexible, you will struggle in your effort to achieve happiness. Be adaptable and accept the changes.

The process is slow at times but necessary to achieve happiness and peace. Isn't that what we all want? You can have a ton of money and yet be a bitter, lonely man. Do not be that person. It is paramount you believe in yourself throughout this calamity. This is the time you need to find new meaning and purpose for your life.

Ask yourself this fundamental question: "Why was I born?" Write it down and say it aloud. You will be amazed at how this will make you feel. Announce to the universe, "I am entitled to love, happiness and success." Be proud to be a man.

This book illustrates the mistakes I made, but my flawed relationships were not a waste of time. I am glad for all the experiences, good and bad. They helped me realize who I am and appreciate all the things I learned from the women in my life. I would like to take this time to apologize to anyone I have hurt or to whom I have made insensitive comments. It feels good to admit my mistakes and do my best not to repeat them.

It has been over ten years since my divorce and I am at the point in my life where I can barely recognize the person I was when all this started. I feel I have accomplished what I always wanted after my divorce: happiness, closure and a new me.

It's okay to be self-caring and do something for yourself. This is one area where women excel. They go to spas, shopping for shoes, pedicures and experience just about every gratification available, while many men work and pay the bills. Work and paying the bills are important, but so is having fun. I took some dance classes and after I got over my awkward feet, I started to have fun. Dance classes are a great place to meet women and overcome your shyness. Just try it.

From the time I was born until I was thirty-five years old, I had my family, wife, and friends—someone around me nearly all the time. I did not understand what it was like to be completely alone. When I was twenty-seven, I used to take guitar lessons from a complex and insightful man. His name is Chris, and while we were talking one day, he made a very poignant comment. Chris said, "I don't think you realize what it's like to wake up in the morning and be alone."

He lived alone in a small house and could speak from experience. It wasn't making much sense to me until after my divorce and I had moved into this house; then I completely understood what he meant. He told me possibly I planned my life so as not to be alone, and consequently, at times, chose to be with a companion who might not be right for me. Chris is not only a great guitar player, but very intuitive.

Try to be happy when you are alone. One time I was so lonely, wanting someone just to talk to me. Overwhelmed with being alone I started to cry. As the tears came so did the thought I believe to this day, "If I can't find happiness alone, then I *do not* deserve it!" That concept changed my life. It can change yours too. I realize some people do better by themselves than others, but you will need some solitude to sort through the tidal wave of emotions that separation and divorce initiate.

Don't look for a replacement bulb when it is *you* that needs a new string of lights. Tell yourself every day, "I'm going to get through this and become a better and stronger person." If you don't believe it, *say* it until you do. Positive reinforcement is a powerful ally.

Now that my parents are gone, my need for finding closure is more important than ever. They may not be here in the physical sense but I will always carry part of them with me. I have come to terms with my own vulnerabilities and mortality as well as my strength and uniqueness. I am very proud of my parents and their legacy. I strongly recommend establishing and maintaining, as best you can, a healthy relationship with your parents. After divorce, you will need their love and guidance.

IF DIVORCE IS like someone dying, then recovering is like being reborn. A rebirth, if you will, of someone you knew existed but did not know how to bring into the light of a new day. He is in there, but you have to bring him out.

My wish for all men struggling with this crisis is to get to a place where "the new you" has such merit and significance that the old you no longer has any meaning. To the new you, the old you will be an unrecognizable figure as though he were distorted through the lens of a camera, out of focus.

The divorce journey has taken me through many difficult phases. This was necessary for me to evolve into who I am now. I feel I have come from the dark cold shadows and now am illuminated by a warming light— melting the past and embracing the present. Right now is all I have and I choose to be happy. I deserve it! So do all of you.

God bless.... Michael Louis Eads

WORKS CITED

Collins, Phil. 1981. In The Air Tonight. [prod.] Phil Collins and Hugh Padgham. *Face Value.* s.l. : Atlantic Records, 1981.

Seger, Bob and The Silver Bullet Band. 1982. Shame On The Moon. [prod.] Jimmy Lovine. *The Distance.* s.l. : Capitol Records, 1982.

The Allman Brothers Band. 1972. [prod.] Tom Dowd. *Eat a Peach.* s.l. : Capicorn Records, 1972.

Wikipedia. [Online] http://www.wikipedia.org.

ABOUT THE AUTHOR

Michael Eads loves the written word. He lives with his wife and dog near Seattle, Washington. He believes that: "New emotions are born from 'the process.' When men go through crisis and tragedy, unfamiliar feelings are summoned and our character is redefined. When we meet these challenges head on and accept the changes we must go through, we discover one more characteristic, integrity."

CPSIA information can be obtained
at www.ICGtesting.com
Printed in the USA
LVHW01s0436230818
587869LV00001B/34/P

9 780979 848438